End of Life Planning Book for

_____
By: Leslie Cottrell Simonds

Copyright © 2016 by Leslie Cottrell Simonds, All rights reserved. No part of this book may be reproduced in any form without the written permission of the author and its publisher.

Table of Contents

Introduction 18
How To Use This Book 23
Basic Information 28
Banking, Insurances 38
Sources of Income and Business Interests 49
Assets, Investments, IRA's and Annuities 56
Online Presence 64
Power of Attorney, Advance Directives and Wills 71
Beloved Pets 90
Gifts 100
End of Life Care 104
Information for After Death 114
After Death Care and Family Led Death care 138
Funeral and Memorial Wishes 155
Eulogy Notes 169
Life Inventory 191
Personal Notes 195

Acknowledgements

I believe it is safe to say the first seeds of this book were sown during the lengthy illness of my Father. There were many times as he lost his ability to communicate with us through words that I wondered if we were doing all we could to uphold what he would want. I am thankful to have journeyed that time alongside my Mother who clearly knew Dad better than anyone. Even so, I know Mom would agree that there were moments when we second guessed ourselves. The times of uncertainty made my mind wander to those that face a serious illness of a loved one without knowing what their wishes would be. For that and so many more life lessons, I thank my Father for his inspiration.

For the assistance of my Daughter in all of the practical aspects of formatting a book and keeping things looking good, I am ever thankful. How wonderful to have a cracker jack virtual assistant in the family. I am doubly blessed to have a Daughter and Son who so believe in their mother!

Nina Thompson of the WakeUpToDyingProject.org has been invaluable as a sounding board and guide when I decided to take a simple but lengthy form and make it into this book you hold in your hands. Thank you Nina for all your input!

It has been my honor to be involved in the forming of a small group of women in Massachusetts called "Home Funeral Friends". We came together because of the wonderful, talented, and loving Peg Lorenz of PeacefulPassageAtHome.com. For over seven years, Peg has been helping families desiring an opportunity to reclaim the healing journey of caring for their own dead at home. With an increasing interest in family led death care, Peg felt the time was perfect to bring others in to help with education and family assistance. Being a part of this newly formed group only served to enhance the words of this book, and for that I thank each member of our little clan.

Denise Brown of Caregiving.com with whom I studied to become a certified caregiving consultant was a wonderful support at just the right time. It's great when a cheerleader comes along when you need one the most. My studies with Denise re-affirmed that the end of life chapter along the journey of caregiving is really where my passions lie, and I am most grateful for her friendship and guidance.

I Want You to Know

I thank my Mother for her insightful "knowing" that a book was coming. It was never a question of if, but only a question of when. She reminds me every now and then that my first love was always writing. Her unfaltering care of my father was a shining example of love in action through every day of his illness.

I am ever thankful for the ongoing support and presence of my Brother. Though he was living far away during the years of my Dad's illness, he was always there at least in spirit and certainly only a phone call away. He listened to my concerns, my vents, my grief, and it never mattered the time of day. The few times when I sounded the alarm for him to come, he'd be on the next flight he could make. He had a powerful and comforting way of being around us even from a distance. For that, I will always be overflowing with gratitude.

Through the power of creative and energetic women coming together to learn and to influence the future of business, marketing, and communication, I connected with the vivacious and masterful marketing strategist, Jennifer Kem. I became a part of a group of professional women who infuse the WOW factor into their entrepreneurial ventures. In that group, I learned of the talents of Kathy and Steve Kidd of Kidd Marketing. They took this fledgling author under their wing and together, we are soaring. Many, many thanks!

I also was given encouragement and great advice back in the earlier days of the book from my beautiful gifted niece, Rivera Sun. Rivera is the author of The Dandelion Insurrection, and The Billionaire Buddha, just to name two of her books. Her bold journey down the self-publishing road serves as a great inspiration to me.

For Natalie and Tanya from Studio at 13, and Kimberly of Kimberly Jones Photography, I don't know how you did it, but you ladies actually made me look presentable for the cover photo. Thanks for all your primping and for being so darn fun along the way!

Cathy Cartisano Andrews of Wings on the Ground, my Spiritual Sister, has been invaluable to me both in friendship and knowledge. Cathy was the first person to affirm that my intuition was spot on regarding how I was led to uphold my Father in his final journey. Without that, who knows? This work may have never been started.

For all the stories that were lovingly shared with me to use for illustration purposes, I am forever grateful. People whose lives have been forever changed through their experiences with loss that wasn't planned for; came forward to tell their story. Whether presented here as a compilation or singularly, these experiences help us learn and feel the importance of the power of planning. I am so grateful for the generosity of so many to help others.

But most of all, my thanks and gratitude go to my dearest friend and love, Bob Simonds. Without his support emotionally, personally and financially, I would not have had the opportunity to create this book and pursue the field of end of life care. His unfailing belief in my passions and abilities is hard for me to comprehend. He has truly taught me what it means to be in a partnership for life. Bob, you are beyond, "the best".

Foreword

Back in 2000, my Father couldn't put off knee replacement surgery any longer. In those days, my parents were living on their own, and overall, still fairly healthy. Back then, I didn't intervene much in health care decisions. My Father had undergone several hernia operations and a heart valve replacement, but I'd never felt the uncomfortable nervousness I was feeling as the day of the knee surgery came closer. I asked more exploratory questions than I had in the past and even had a few extra questions that I asked my Mother to get answered by Dad's primary care physician. The feeling of nervousness continued, but Dad was more and more uncomfortable every week. It was evident in the disruption of his normally energetic activity level. Clearly the surgery was called for.

During times of my Dad's hospitalizations, I always tried to be present in his hospital room as much as possible. Both of my parents were of strong mind at this stage, but my conviction is that everyone needs an advocate when they are hospitalized. My trust level of hospital staff has always been tenuous. I've seen too many accidents, too many slip ups, and too much complacency amongst hospital staff through the years to feel comfortable without having an advocate present for my Father to serve as a sounding board and extra support for my Mother.

I have friends that are doctors, nurses, and social workers.

Nonetheless, I simply do not trust things to automatically go according to the best interest of a family member when they are under the care of hospitals.

Having a "go to" person that is consistently present through the change of doctors on call, nurse's shifts, and lab personnel assures that one person is hearing all the courses of treatment, prescribed medicines, treatments, etc.

I was fortunate at that time to be working on the same hospital campus where my Dad was to have his surgery. My schedule could temporarily be fluid enough for me to come and go throughout the day which allowed me to be with him a good amount of time when things like doctors' rounds and meals where happening.

I Want You to Know

The day arrived for Dad's surgery and everything went as planned according to his surgeon. We waited patiently for him to come out of anesthesia and be brought back to his room. When he was returned from the recovery room, we immediately knew something was off. Because of Dad's former surgical procedures, I knew what he acted like as he came out of anesthesia. This was an abnormal response, and there it was.... the sick sinking feeling that my intuitive premonition was coming true. There seemed to be an odd cloud between Dad and reality. It wasn't profound enough for the health care team to notice the difference immediately, because they didn't know pre-surgery Dad well enough.

My Father was noticeably confused, and agitated. He was struggling to follow even the simplest instructions. I could write an entire book dedicated to the outcome of this surgery, believe it or not, even including a bout of never ending hiccups that lasted almost a week. Nothing the doctors tried worked.

It was beyond irritating to see how dismissive everyone was of the effects on Dad to have those constant deep hiccups. Imagine trying to eat and trying to sleep with hiccups. Day after day we asked the nurses and doctors to make note of our concerns in Dad's chart. I knew something had happened while he was in surgery. My fear had come true, and what we were seeing was real. We were feeling unheard and frustrated when we tried to voice our concerns over Dad's mental state. The feeling of being out of control is never an enjoyable one. We were juggling all the pieces: pain management, issues with bladder catheterization, lack of appetite, uncontrolled hiccups and what appeared to be mild dementia symptoms. Personally, in addition, I had to add staying on top of my job, being a single parent of two teenage children, and the added hours in my Dad's hospital room. It was a frustrating and frightening few weeks.

As the days progressed, Dad was neither physically nor mentally improving much. Our frustration mounted, and I felt like a broken record each day as I stated what we were seeing and asked, "Please include our observations in my father's chart." What was to be a three to four-day hospital stay turned into 14 or more; time has blurred some of the details. When Dad was finally bumped up to rehab, he was still exhibiting some confusion although it seemed to be lessening.

I Want You to Know

I was so frustrated that no one could tell us what may have happened while he was in surgery. Finally, late in his hospital stay, just before Dad left for rehab, one of the doctors did admit that he may have suffered some kind "allergic reaction" to anesthesia. That was all we got at the time. After the fact, when I had time to start researching, I came across a definition of vascular dementia, and felt I had come upon an explanation. I began asking his doctors and other doctors questions but still got little further information. Although evidence would suggest that receiving general anesthesia does not increase the likelihood of developing lasting vascular dementia, recent experiments on both animal and human cells show that anesthesia can increase the buildup of the proteins thought to underlie dementia, especially in higher doses. Was that what happened in Dad's case? We will never know for sure.

There were more than a few times I told my Mother that the time would come when we would look back and pinpoint that surgery as a turning point. Skip ahead more than a decade to the day that Mom and Dad sat in a neurologist's office well after Dad had been tested several times for Alzheimer's. They heard the doctor use the term "vascular dementia" for the very first time. The oddest part was that the neurologist said it in such a way that he seemed a bit surprised that he was the first one that had used the term with them. Oh, how I wish I had been present for THAT doctor's visit!

But at that point, it was really too late. Dad progressed medically as well as mentally to the point that he was not able to be home any longer. His physical care became too much for my Mom to handle. Following a cardiac event, Dad had to undergo a permanent catheterization. In addition to his failing mental condition, the care required to maintain his catheter would be far more than my aging Mother could handle on her own. With broken hearts, we had to admit that Dad would never be returning home.

Looking back on my Father's journey, I wondered if we could have done things differently. I wondered if we could have done better by him. I know that question is not unusual. There were many times along the way when I questioned what Dad would have wanted if he could have spoken for himself. I just never thought about having the tough conversations with him back when I still could. I was naive and hoping for the best. What child wants to think about the mortality of their parents? I turned myself inside out emotionally for a long time after the death of my Father as I pondered if I did enough. I know my Mother had many of the same concerns. The answer is, yes, we did

I Want You to Know

enough; yes, we were the best advocates possible. I now have complete peace with the role I played in Dad's care. It took me a long time to get there, but I know that we did the best that we could with the tools that we had.

The first days, weeks, and months following the death of a loved one are a bitter cocktail of feelings; feeling that everything is surreal and at the same time feeling extreme emotional pain and confusion. But even then, in those early days after Dad's death, I was sitting with a new awareness about myself and about helping others face their end of life journey with support.

Before being by my father's side as he left this life, I had been with a number of people in their last days and moments. I'd found myself with those transitioning in the days I was an EMT, also as an Executive Chef in a high end retirement facility, and also with a former partner's mother. It was a poignant but comfortable place for me to be. I didn't know that it wasn't particularly "normal" to feel honored and blessed to be in the presence of someone who was crossing over to their next adventure. I didn't know that most people are frightened to be with someone who is dying. For me, it always felt completely normal. It felt like I was exactly where I should be.

When my Father's primary care physician told my Mother that Dad had not much more than a week to live, I told my boss that I would be leaving for an undetermined amount of time. He knew why. We'd talked about my father's condition and I had told him I'd be leaving to be by my dad's side when the time came.

Although there had been plenty of time to prepare, I drove the 90 minutes to Dad's bedside in a fog. I only knew my goal was to be present, to support my Father's final journey. Beyond that, I had no idea what to expect. Ironically, at this same time, my Mother suffered a cardiac event. I think she had just reached her limit. Suddenly I had two parents in serious medical condition in hospitals 45 minutes apart. Whichever parent I was with, I felt I was in the wrong place. Fortunately, Mom's condition turned out to be fairly minor, and I was able to take her back to be with my Father after a couple of days. I was grateful to be able to be there and close at hand, especially now that Mom needed to be home just a little more than usual while she recovered.

I found myself doing things from intuition that I felt were just the right thing for my Dad even though he was mostly unresponsive. Sometime after my Father's death, I learned from a friend that teaches death midwifery that the things I had done for Dad were the very things she teaches to her students. "Where did those ideas come from?" she asked. Being able to say that they came to me, intuitively, made me realize that I may be naturally suited to hold sacred space for those that are preparing for their journey to the other side. Perhaps that was why I had been in the presence of so many people as they prepared to leave their bodies.

So began my journey to learn more about how to best serve those that are facing this life's last journey. As I launched my consulting business, I felt equally drawn to support those that serve as caregivers. Caregiving is one of life's most challenging tasks, and the toll it can take is rarely acknowledged. Much like talking about death, we don't like to talk about the sacrifice of caregiving. It makes us uncomfortable; it takes us to a place we don't want to visit so we avoid it.

We avoid it until it is sitting beside us in the room and there is no longer any escape. Sometimes it comes in like a freight train, and we find ourselves instantly thrown into a new world we are simply not prepared for. Sometimes it flirts around the edges like a shadow we barely see out of the corner of our eye. Bit by bit, it comes closer, more into focus, and then, there it is: we are caregivers.

How do we know we are doing what our loved one would want? How do we know what their wishes would be regarding life support, CPR, tube feeding? How do we know what they would want for their final disposition? There are just so many questions, many we would never think to ask ahead of time. Frequently when the time arrives to provide the answers, it's too late to get them from the source. What then? We wing it, we talk among our siblings and rarely is there a consensus. Many families fall apart under the pressure of these intense times of having to decide right now. I started looking for a resource to find all those questions listed in one form. What I found were checklists that provided the opportunity to record bits and pieces of the journey through life threatening illness, or for the final funeral and body disposition process. Nowhere did I find one document that asked all the questions I was looking for in one place.

I decided to do what any self-respecting Aries, Type-A personality would do: create my own! That was the catalyst for this book. Within these pages

I Want You to Know

you will find just about every question you could ever imagine and many you probably would never think of. I recommend starting this process early and taking it slow. The best time to prepare is well before an emergency.

I encourage you to not become overwhelmed by some of the questions. You may be tempted to skip over some parts or just set the whole book aside. Please don't do that! Take your time to ponder and even do some research, but do answer all the questions. You can always go back and change answers later if your perspective changes.

This provides a great opportunity for discussion among your family members for their ideas and opinions. Some of these concepts may be new to them as well. One of the interesting outcomes from this exercise will be knowing yourself better when you are finished with this book than before you started. No doubt, you'll know your family members better as you discuss these important questions.

My husband brought an important question to me just as I was almost finished writing this book. He asked what I was going to do to support those that don't enjoy reading, and especially don't enjoy filling out forms (I'm not actually sure that anyone enjoys filling out forms!). How would people like that (meaning him!), have the opportunity to express their wishes? It set a great deal of conversation in motion, and we are still working on ideas. If you are the personality type that falls into that category, feel free to send me an email:leslie@thevisionarypassage.com. My talented VA and I are working together to create an easily approachable way to capture your information.

You may wonder, "Why is there a tractor on your book cover? My father had a deep passion for farming and for restoring old tractors. He always had a tractor or two out in his barn in various stages of repair. This old John Deere felt like the perfect backdrop for my photo. It felt great to bring one more little part of Dad along for another leg of the journey.

Introduction

In the last five years, I've been amazed to see the barriers surrounding conversations about end of life issues begin to soften. Two years ago, I suggested to a group I was studying with that within the next five years we would see a major shift in the way most people view death and the death process. Those that had been in the field of elder care, hospice, and home funeral education all said, "Oh no! That's far too soon. We've started the shift, but it will be a few decades before people alter their view of death." Now, just two short years later, I am amazed at the growth in how the general public has started shifting into an acceptance of open discussion. Death Cafes are increasingly filled to capacity, and educational tools like Nina Thompson's "Wake Up to Dying Project" are gaining more public attention all the time.

One of the powerful attributes of the baby boomer generation is the drive to create their own experiences by breaking down barriers and smashing molds of the status quo throughout all their life cycles. Natural childbirth was a movement that went from the hippy culture to the main stream in what seemed like a hot minute. This generation has continued to redefine all the phases of life on their terms. Yoga, Kirtan, and meditation are all expressions of spiritual practice that were virtually unknown to the mainstream population 20 years ago. So too, seeking out celebrants to perform weddings, baby blessings and funerals have exploded in just the last 5-10 years. We are no longer satisfied with just going through the motions for the big events in life.

How many flat cookie cutter funerals have you attended? Performed with the best of intentions, clergy present a 20-30 minute service that many times includes the same prayers, all the usual scripture reading, and a eulogy that could have been scripted from the newspaper obituary. I've come away from those kinds of funerals feeling empty that the person had not been appropriately remembered for the life they had lived. Conversely, a celebrant (or an engaged and creative clergy person) will interview family and friends to really capture the essence of the deceased. The celebration of life will many times leave the attendees feeling that they know the deceased better than they did before the service. These services frequently include a ritual that embraces all who attend and draws them into an experiential way of expressing their grief. These are but a few of the changes for the better for this aging generation of baby boomers and the next to come.

The next frontier is applying the same passion and individuality to the planning of our death journey. Think about it for a moment. If you had the opportunity to express your wishes for the final days of your life, wouldn't you like to do that? The physiological symptoms of the death process reflect a journey of separation. The soul begins to separate from the body as we become less attached to the earthly plane. Because of that process, we won't be having in-depth conversations with our loved ones at that point. Knowing that, doesn't it make sense to document what you think you would like for comfort care during those days?

Let's try a short experiment. Think about being at your most stressed after a perfect storm of a day. What brings you comfort, what calms you, what relaxes you? It may be poetry, a special playlist of music, fresh air, a massage; but chances are you have your own go-to for your most stressful days. It is those methods of self-comfort care that you would also benefit from as you enter the states of bodily transition during the death process. The difference is, you won't be able to provide those things for yourself at that time. These are the ideas and wishes you can now capture and have documented for your loved ones to refer to should you become ill.

All we are doing throughout this book is projecting ahead to the days when we may not be able to speak for ourselves, when we may not be able to communicate. It's important that you have the opportunity to be comforted in the ways that work best for you. It truly is a loving act to share these ideas with those that will be looking after you.

Wouldn't you be relieved and supported to know exactly what your loved one most wanted for care as they were dying? Wouldn't you feel that a great deal of pressure was taken off your shoulders to know what your loved one wanted for a celebration of their life and not have to guess or design it yourself when you were already immersed in grief? Here is your tool to do the same thing for your family and friends. Don't stop there! Make sure your parents, aunts, uncles, brothers, and sisters all do the same for themselves and their families.

What happens when you create a death plan and then change your mind? I recommend that this document be reviewed yearly to make sure that everything listed here is still in alignment with your wishes. Your birthday is

I Want You to Know

the perfect annual reminder to page through the book and make any adjustments necessary.

Lastly, what if your death plan is no longer working for you? As mentioned before, the body, mind, and spirit are all undergoing major transitions during the death process. Have conversations well in advance with those that will be sitting in vigil with you. Tell them that you are aware that any communicated death plan must stay fluid to allow for changes. This will help your caregiver(s) remain in the moment to support your current condition while respecting your wishes.

When the times comes, they may be able to tell just by your slight expressions that you are no longer enjoying having your feet rubbed with lavender oil or that the music you asked for is not comforting you. Communication is key in all things. The more your loved ones know about your wishes and the more they know you at your essence, the more they will be able to adjust accordingly. As your time of death approaches and your attachment to your surroundings lessen, you may very well simply desire silence.

When my father was close to death, I just knew innately that it was time for silence. I had taken him through a series of changes in the style of music being played in his room for the last 5 days. Suddenly, I had an overwhelming awareness that the time for any music was over. One thing to consider is a non-verbal sign that you wish for all stimuli to stop. I don't have any research to support whether someone can remember to signal at that stage of the death process, although I have heard it discussed. What might you want that signal to be? A tapping in your loved ones' palm, an extension of your index finger on the bed? If you want to at least leave this open as an option, be sure to be very clear with those that will be with you.

Another option that may be more practical would be to request in advance that as your symptoms reach those of someone in their final hours that there be silence in the vigil room. A few symptoms caregivers will want to watch for in the last few hours are: irregular breathing (otherwise known as Cheyne-Stokes respiration), very slow respirations, unresponsiveness, eyes either half closed or open but without focus, lips and nail beds a blueish color, fluid in the back of the throat causing what is known as the "death rattle", hands and feet a mottled purplish color that begins to spread. I do recommend that you do your own research on these final signs and symptoms to be more familiar with the final stages of dying.

An interesting fact is that 100% of us will die. That's reason enough to think about what we would like our deaths to look like, isn't it? Only about 10% of deaths are completely unexpected as in death by trauma or unexpected medical emergency. 90% of all the people reading this book will know for at least a short time that their death is coming. I can't speak for you, but I feel strongly that I'd like my family to already know how I'd like to be cared for at the end of my life, and how I'd like my body cared for after death. I bet that many of you feel the same way. End of life planning is love in action. What do you choose for your legacy?

Not only is end of life planning an active gift of love, it may also be our final gift of love. We've worked diligently all our lives to grow up and make our way in the world as productive people pursuing our passions and making a living. We went on to raise our children to be better versions of who we have been by teaching them to think, allowing them to stretch as people and know themselves well, and to be kind and caring for those around them and to live well. Does it not make good sense that we can also teach our children and our children's children how to die well? Why should we cease to be the best example of a life well lived before we die?

As I have aged into my 50's and my children share stories with me about wounds they suffered as children (all children have them!), I realize that, although I feel I did a pretty good job overall as a parent, there are definitely some things that I could have done better. I could have been more expansive at times, and allowed life's circumstances to be opportunities for learning and growth. Instead, because I was working excessive hours to support my children and the commodity of time always seemed to be short, I know there were days that I tried to just "get through" a challenge so that I could move forward with the unending daily task list. My goal is to be as intentional in my death as is possible. I deeply desire that process to serve as the final good example to my beloved family. I desire "love in action" to be my legacy.

How To Use This Book

This book is meant to not only be read, but also to be utilized! Just reading it may give you some great ideas, but if you don't do the work and fill in the pages, no one will ever know the things you most want to share.

At first glance it may look like a huge project, and like most huge projects, the hardest part is actually getting started. I recommend that you read through the pages to understand what is included and to research some of the sections that you may be unfamiliar with.

Next, instead of setting it aside with the good intention of filling some of it out at a later time, go ahead and set your timer for just 30 minutes. Open up the basic information section and fill it out. You are just entering the names and contact information of your family members. Easy, right? Now go ahead and skip around a little if you like. Grab a few sections that feel less intimidating and finish out the 30 minutes on your timer. If that feels like enough for one day, put it aside. If you feel ready for more.... keep on going!

The section on Assets, Insurances, Income from Investments, etc., may be tedious, but not particularly emotionally taxing, so consider doing those next. Again, set a timer for 15-30 minutes and stop when the timer goes off. If you feel like you want to keep going after that, go right ahead. Once all that information is documented, you can move on to the sections that are going to force you to dig a little deeper.

Download your state specific forms for Power of Attorney, Advanced Directive, Designated Agent, and MOLST or POLST (these are only for an already advanced medical condition), and finally 5 Wishes. These all must be signed and witnessed to be legally binding. There are still 8 states that do not recognize 5 wishes as a legal form, so check your state's status. After filling the forms out and having them witnessed as required per each form, decide if you want to attach copies to the book, or have them stored in another place. Be sure to designate within this book where the forms are to be found.

The questions within these medical forms are probably the most challenging of all. Medical questions about your care after a life threatening illness or injury can be very stressful to ponder. Taking charge of your own life and destiny is empowering and well worth the discomfort. Just remember that the discomfort is temporary, but the benefits will be long lasting. You need to be specific here for a reason. Just saying that you wish or don't wish for extraordinary measures does not really do much to help a trauma team or your primary care physician, now does it? Let's look at one aspect of extra ordinary measures: feeding tubes. How you feel about the use of a feeding tube may be vastly different at 51 then it will be at 81. Answer each question as if it would need to be answered right now, not in 30 years. Now if you think about the temporary use of a feeding tube would you feel differently? Would you want it to be reexamined if you still needed it after 8 weeks if you didn't have brain activity?

The final piece will be recording your stories. I believe it is a lovely way to finish out your journey through this book. Take your time with this section and allow time to come back and continue to add stories as new things come to mind. The documentation of your life story is going to be cherished by your family members. Imagine your children and your children's children reading these stories for years to come. I wish I had this for each of my grandparents and my own parents. Much like turning the pages in old photo albums, reading these snapshots of your life will keep history alive for generations to come.

Be prepared for things to surface as you work your way through this book. Be on the lookout for resistance as you do this personal excavation. Our ego is such a funny thing. Our ego-self really does not like change and growth. It is most comfortable with the status quo. Whenever we stretch ourselves and step into our own truth, the ego can freak out and begin to do a number on us. You may start having thoughts such as, "This work is stupid." "No one is going to care what I write here." "This is a waste of time." "Who is ever going to read this?" You can be sure that the more of these thoughts you have and the more challenged your ego is feeling, the more important it is to forge ahead! I can tell you, those same thoughts snuck in while I was writing this book. This is an opportunity to learn more about yourself and how you feel about some of the really important things in your life. Don't let it pass you by. If you are reading these words, this book has come to you for a reason. Be bold. Start creating your legacy right now.

Thank you for being a change maker. It is people like you who are altering the face of death, and removing the stigma of discussion and planning for a good death. Pre-planning is truly love in action.

One final note about the stories you will read about other people's personal experiences throughout this book. My desire was to illustrate the outcome that both having plans in place and not having plans in place has on those that are left behind after a death. Names have been changed in all these stories to be sensitive to the privacy of other family members involved.

I Want You to Know

"No one wants to die.

Even people who want to go to heaven don't want to die to get there.

And yet death is the destination we all share. No one has ever escaped it. And that is as it should be, because death is very likely the single best invention of life. It is life's change agent. It clears out the old to make way for the new. Right now the new is you, but someday not too long from now, you will gradually become the old and be cleared away. Sorry to be so dramatic, but it is quite true."

~~Steve Jobs

I Want You to Know

Basic Information

Let's begin with the easy information! This chapter is all about the basics. Be as complete as possible as you work through each chapter, but especially so in the basic information chapter. As we move on, things get a little more involved. The reason this information is important to your family is that they need basic information to distribute your estate and potentially for other arrangements after you die. Former addresses are important if family members need to locate documents that were created in other states or counties. It's alright if you don't remember entire address; just list what you do remember. Try to place dates as close as you can remember when you have lived at other addresses.

<u>REMINDER: This workbook is for your personal planning and communication purposes. This document whether hard copy or digital is not mean to be substituted for any legal or medical document. The creation of the document is not to be construed as either or medical advice.</u>

Basic Information:

Name:
_____
Address:
_____
Phone:
_____
Secondary Phone:
_____
Email:
_____
Full Maiden Name:
_____
Birthplace:
_____

Former Addresses and Dates of Residence:

_____

_____

_____

_____

_____

_____

_____

_____

Spouse/Partner/Other

Name:
_____

Relationship:
_____

Address:
_____

City, State, Zip:
_____

Phone:
_____

Email:
_____

I Want You to Know

Child:

Name:
_____

Address:
_____

City, State, Zip:
_____

Phone:
_____

Email:
_____

Child:

Name:
_____

Address:
_____

City, State, Zip:
_____

Phone:
_____

Email:
_____

Child:

Name:
_____

Address:
_____

City, State, Zip:
_____

Phone:
_____

Email:
_____

Child:

Name:
_____

Address:
_____

City, State, Zip:
_____

Phone:
_____

Email:
_____

Child:

Name:
_____

Address:
_____

City, State, Zip:
_____

Phone:
_____

Email:
_____

Deceased Relatives:

Name:
_____

DOB: _____ DOD: _____

Name:
_____

DOB: _____ DOD: _____

I Want You to Know

Name:
_____

DOB: _____ DOD: _____

Name:
_____

DOB: _____ DOD: _____

Name:
_____

DOB: _____ DOD: _____

Name:
_____

DOB: _____ DOD: _____

Name:
_____

DOB: _____ DOD: _____

Name:
_____

DOB: _____ DOD: _____

Name:
_____

DOB: _____ DOD: _____

Name:
_____

DOB: _____ DOD: _____

I Want You to Know

Papers and Essential Data:

Review paperwork periodically to update, make sure beneficiaries are accurate, etc. Determine if your survivors will have easy access to your accounts after death.

Location of:

Address Book:
_____

Children's Records:
_____

Birth Certificates:
_____

Immunization:
_____

Marriage/Domestic Partnership/Civil Union:
_____

Pre and Post Nuptial Agreements:
_____

Divorce Papers:
_____

Birth Certificates/Adoption Papers:
_____

Military Records:
_____

Voter Registration:
_____

Passport:
_____

Naturalization Papers:
_____

Past Tax Returns and Supporting Data:
_____

I Want You to Know

Court documents that could lay claim to my estate:

_____

_____

_____

_____

Other:
_____

Copyrights/Patents:
_____

Frequent Flyer Miles (transferrable):
_____

Household Inventory:
_____

Note if attached here:
_____

Keys

Post Office Box:
_____

Car/Truck/Boat/RV:
_____

Safe Deposit Box:
_____

Safe:
_____

House:
_____

Home Safe

Location of Safe:
_____

Location of Key or Combination:
_____

Storage Unit

Name of Company:
_____

Address:
_____

City, State, Zip:
_____

Phone:
_____

I Want You to Know

*"At the end of the day, the only questions
I will ask myself are...
Did I love enough? Did I laugh enough?
Did I make a difference?"*

~~*Unknown*

I Want You to Know

Banking, Insurances

Here we will designate all banking information. Many of us have multiple accounts in multiple banks. Be sure to include everything and keep this section updated as accounts change.

Let's start with your safe deposit box. For some reason, this important item frequently gets forgotten.

Note: An inventory of the contents of your safety deposit box is very helpful in determining the urgency in obtaining an order to open the box. A safe deposit box is not the place to keep your advance directive, health care POA, or other items that will need to be accessed quickly.

Safe Deposit Box

Name of Institution:
_____

Address:
_____

Phone Number:
_____

Box Number: _____ Location of Key: _____

Inventory of contents of box:

_____

_____

_____

_____

_____

_____

Name of Bank/Credit Union:

Address:
_____

City, State, Zip:
_____

Phone:
_____

Type of Account:
_____

Account Number:
_____

Name of Bank/Credit Union:

Address:
_____

City, State, Zip:
_____

Phone:
_____

Type of Account:
_____

Account Number:
_____

Name of Bank/Credit Union:

Address:
_____

City, State, Zip:
_____

Phone:
_____

Type of Account:
_____

Account Number:
_____

I use online banking: _____

The following bills are paid automatically from my account:

_____

_____

_____

_____

_____

_____

Insurances

Homeowners/Renter's Insurance Company:
_____

Address:
_____

City, State, Zip:
_____

Phone:
_____

Insurance Agent (if applicable):
_____

Location of Policy:
_____

Automotive Insurance Company:
_____

Address:
_____

City, State, Zip:
_____

Phone:
_____

Insurance Agent (if applicable):
_____

Location of Policy:
_____

Medical Insurance Company:
_____

Address:
_____

City, State, Zip:
_____

Phone:
_____

Insurance Agent (if applicable):
_____

Location of Policy:
_____

Dental Insurance Company:
_____

Address:
_____

City, State, Zip:
_____

Phone:
_____

Insurance Agent (if applicable):
_____

Location of Policy:
_____

Long Term Care Insurance Company:
_____

Address:
_____

City, State, Zip:
_____

Phone:
_____

I Want You to Know

Insurance Agent (if applicable):
_____

Location of Policy:
_____

Professional Insurance Company:
_____

Address:
_____

City, State, Zip:
_____

Phone:
_____

Insurance Agent (if applicable):
_____

Location of Policy:
_____

Liability Insurance Company:
_____

Address:
_____

City, State, Zip:
_____

Phone:
_____

Insurance Agent (if applicable):
_____

Location of Policy:
_____

Disability Insurance Company:
_____

Address:
_____

City, State, Zip:
_____

Phone:
_____

Insurance Agent (if applicable):
_____

Location of Policy:
_____

Life Insurance Company:
_____

Address:
_____

City, State, Zip:
_____

Phone:
_____

Policy Number:
_____

Death Benefit:
_____

Outstanding Loan Amount (if applicable):
_____

Beneficiary:
_____

Location of Policy:
_____

Insurance Agent (if applicable):
_____

Life Insurance Company (2nd Policy):
_____

Address:
_____

City, State, Zip:
_____

Phone:
_____

Policy Number:
_____

Death Benefit:
_____

I Want You to Know

Outstanding Loan Amount (if applicable):
_____

Location of Policy:
_____

Insurance Agent (if applicable):
_____

A Daughter's Plea

One of the most poignant interviews I had for this book was with a woman who I have had the pleasure of getting to know through her work as a coach. She is one of those truly blessed people who had a very close relationship with both her mother and stepfather. Beverly refers to her step father as her guardian angel. Her mother died unexpectedly in 2007. Even if her mother's death had not been unexpected, Beverly does not believe her mother was the type of person who would have ever put a death plan in place. It simply was not in keeping with who she was. Her Mom was a true minimalist; living off the grid. Settling her estate was relatively easy in terms of modern day comparison, but that did not lessen the deep impact that it had on both Beverly and her sister.

The immediate responsibilities of decision making regarding her mother's final disposition were literally more than she could bear to face. Beverly remembers sitting in the funeral home doubled over with nausea and resenting every question that was asked of her. It didn't matter that they were basic, straightforward questions. They were questions that no one riding in the tornado of fresh grief should have to ever think about, much less talk about. She described experiencing an overwhelming anger at having to think and talk about decisions as being literally palpable to her.

The entire process of settling her mother's estate, or in Beverly's words, "Closing out her mother's life," took only a few weeks. During this phase, Beverly again was irritated and angry at having to answer questions asked by the people in charge of her mother's accounts. She would become outwardly angry and then direct that anger toward the people she did not want to have to communicate with.

She could barely function through her own personal care, which is as it should be after a death. You should have the right to do nothing but sit, walk, eat, and sleep after the death of someone close to you. Beverly compares it to being a brand new mother. In a perfect world, the new mother should have to do nothing but nurse her baby, feed herself, and rest. Sadly, in our society, that isn't how it works, and it doesn't usually work that way with death either.

Beverly's sister went into hyper-productive mode after the loss of their mother, and that was a great help. Later, it was her turn to help when her sister was ready for relief. Eight years later when their Step-Father died, it was Beverly who took over the role of hyper-productive mode. There was a significant difference between the two experiences. She took it upon herself to have conversations with her Step-Father before his death about what his wishes were. She assured him that the questions were born out of her love and admiration for him. She wanted to show her love and respect for him by assuring that he would be honored in exactly the way that he would want. She wanted to be sure that all his wishes would be respected. Beverly was quick to add that being able to follow a death plan made nothing about his loss any easier to bear. What it did allow was a freedom for the sisters to mourn the loss of their Step-Father fully. They didn't have to shift their focus into pragmatic decisions unlike their experience after their Mother's death.

Beverly feels incredibly sorry for anyone that has to survive the loss of a loved one when there is no death plan in place. "Planning for your final days, for your final disposition, and your earthly belongings is a true act of love", she said. She knows that parents and spouses don't set out to hurt the people they love and have left behind, but the lack of planning does exactly that. It hurts those that suddenly have to make huge decisions when they are at their most vulnerable and least able to think clearly. Beverly went on to tell me, "Communicating a plan for your death is your final gift to your loved ones."

Both Beverly and her sister have taken their experiences to heart. They each have clearly documented wishes for their end of life and their final disposition. Beverly closed our conversation by saying, "Surviving a death of someone close to you releases an emotional avalanche. It will smother you in every way. Just plan ahead so your loved ones can focus on their own journey down the mountain".

I Want You to Know

*"If you want to bring happiness to the whole world,
go home and love your family."*

~~Mother Teresa

Sources of Income and Business Interests

As we journey through our income producing years and beyond, we potentially will have multiple sources of income. It is important for your loved ones to understand not only all your sources of income, but how to access accounts and sources. It is surprising to think that spouses sometimes have no idea where the money in their marriage comes from.

Will grew up in a household that never spoke about money. His parents emigrated from Germany before he was born, and though he tried to get them to talk about their struggles when they first came to the United States, they were not willing to share their stories of the time before he was born. He never knew hunger, but throughout his childhood, his parents acted as though each meal may be their last. Every penny was accounted for and there was never any sort of luxury spending. Christmas was a sparse holiday with trees cut from the woods, handmade strings of popcorn and cranberries, and gifts were few and practical in nature. He told his wife when they were dating that he always felt a sense of fear in his chest as a kid. He felt it all the time like something dreadful was about to happen. He loved his parents deeply, but their legacy was one of fear and lack based on their former experiences that they could not seem to escape.

As Will entered adulthood, he was determined to forge his way in this world with a new attitude. He did well in school and attended college on a full scholarship. However, he always found it frustrating that, try as he might, he just couldn't shake the feeling of fear that his money would run out. Will's wife Clara stopped working when their first child was born and concentrated her efforts on raising their children, keeping the home running, and volunteer work. She really didn't mind that Will was uncommunicative about their finances because it was an aspect of life that she never really enjoyed anyway. Will was obsessed with increasing their savings and was continually finding new ways to invest and deepen their nest egg, but Clara knew none of the specifics. Sadly, it turned out though Will spent a great deal of energy on expanding their savings, it had not reaped much reward, as he invested in things that were too high risk always trying to make money quickly. Looking back Clara thinks that Will was ashamed that he was unable to create that one big score with his investments so he got caught up in a pattern of hiding everything financially related from everyone.

I Want You to Know

When Will died unexpectedly of heart failure in his late 40's, his family's world was suddenly turned upside down. After Clara's return from the hospital that first night, her head was spinning with grief and fear. As her mind raced, the fear outweighed the grief she was feeling. She had no idea about whether Will even had life insurance outside of what his job may have provided, she didn't know if he had a will; she only knew she didn't have one. Was there paperwork somewhere in his den? Where did he keep that kind of information?

Unable to sleep, Clara went down to Will's den and tried to open his desk. It was locked. After rifling through everything on his desk, and the bookshelves, she still had not found a key. She dreaded opening up the bag of Will's things that the hospital had given her, but felt certain that the key to his desk would be on his keyring. It was not. Finally, after going through the cigar box on Will's dresser the next morning, she found a key to open his desk.

The frustration she felt that night just trying to get into her dead husband's desk was just the beginning of a long drawn out journey of discovery. Because Will never felt like he had enough money to spend on things he thought were luxury, he never purchased life insurance beyond the small policy that was a benefit at work. Fortunately, it was enough to bury Will and almost pay off the remaining mortgage on their house. It took almost a year to sort out the different accounts that Will had in his name. After never even balancing a checkbook in decades, Clara was attempting to make sense of accounts she knew nothing of. She sorted through investment statements, many of which were not yielding much money, kept the household running, and attempted to figure out how to find a way to support herself and help her college-age children. To say it was a nightmare is an understatement.

Clara said that the saddest fact of all was that her anger and resentment at having to guess her way through all her husband's paperwork and money trails kept her from grieving him the way she should have been able to grieve. Anger was her primary emotion for almost five years. Finally, she entered counseling to work through her negative emotions.

Her guilt over not having her own will prompted her to see an attorney not long after Will's funeral. She said she never wanted her children to have to be burdened with her lack of planning. She felt blessed to have found an attorney who helped her navigate the waters of settling Will's assets and put a will in place in case something should happen to her before everything was *sorted out with Will's estate. It was a long drawn out affair that she felt put grieving on hold for almost five years.*

~~~~~~

Below you can enter information about your sources of income, and business interests.

Employer:
_____

Address:
_____

City, State, Zip:
_____

Salary/Income:
_____

Employer:
_____

Address:
_____

City, State, Zip:
_____

Salary/Income:
_____

Do you receive Social Security?
_____

Social Security Amount:
_____

Do you receive income from an Annuity Company?
_____

Amount:
_____

Annuity Company Name:
_____

City, State, Zip:
_____

Phone:

I Want You to Know

_____
Do you receive retirement/pension income?
_____
Amount:
_____
Retirement/Pension Employer:
_____
City, State, Zip:
_____

Other Sources of Income:

_____

_____

_____

Business Interests

Name of Business: _____
_____ Sole Proprietor
_____ Corporation
_____ Partnership
_____ LLC

Owners/Partners:
_____
Address:
_____
City, State, Zip:
_____
Phone:
_____

I Want You to Know

Name of Business:
_____

_____ Sole Proprietor
_____ Corporation
_____ Partnership
_____ LLC

Owners/Partners:
_____

Address:
_____

City, State, Zip:
_____

Phone:
_____

Other contracts, partnership or corporate agreements, business interests, etc.:
_____

I Want You to Know

"What feels like the end is often the beginning."

~~Unknown

I Want You to Know

Assets, Investments, IRA's and Annuities

Investments, IRAs, Annuities, Automobiles

For each, list the type (bond, stock, mutual fund, etc.) and location (i.e. in your possession, safe deposit box, or held by a brokerage house).

Type:
_____

Location:
_____

Name of Firm:
_____

Name of Broker:
_____

Address:
_____

City, State, Zip:
_____

Number of Shares:
_____

Approximate Value:
_____

Date of Maturity and possible dates of call:
_____

Type:
_____

Location:
_____

Name of Firm:
_____

Name of Broker:
_____

Address:
_____

City, State, Zip:
_____

Number of Shares:
_____

Approximate Value:
_____

Date of Maturity and possible dates of call:
_____

Type:
_____

Location:
_____

Name of Firm:
_____

Name of Broker:
_____

Address:
_____

City, State, Zip:
_____

Number of Shares:
_____

Approximate Value:
_____

Date of Maturity and possible dates of call:
_____

Type:
_____

Location:
_____

Name of Firm:
_____

Name of Broker:
_____

Address:
_____

City, State, Zip:
_____

I Want You to Know

Number of Shares:

Approximate Value:

Date of Maturity and possible dates of call:

Property

Owner:

Location of title, title search, insurance, bill of sale, etc.:

Amount of Mortgage and Outstanding Principle:

Mortgage Holder:

Address:

City, State, Zip:

Phone:

Owner:

Location of title, title search, insurance, bill of sale, etc.:

Amount of Mortgage and Outstanding Principle:

Mortgage Holder:

Address:

City, State, Zip:

Phone:

Automobiles

Make and Model:
___

Owner:
___

Location of Title:
___

Owner:
___

Location of title, title search, insurance, bill of sale, etc.:
___

Outstanding Loan Amount:
___

Lender:
___

Address:
___

City, State, Zip:
___

Phone:
___

Make and Model:
___

Owner:
___

Location of Title:
___

Owner:
___

Location of title, title search, insurance, bill of sale, etc.:
___

Outstanding Loan Amount:
___

Lender:
___

Address:
___

I Want You to Know

City, State, Zip:
_____

Phone:
_____

Make and Model:
_____

Owner:
_____

Location of Title:
_____

Owner:
_____

Location of title, title search, insurance, bill of sale, etc.:
_____

Outstanding Loan Amount:
_____

Lender:
_____

Address:
_____

City, State, Zip:
_____

Phone:
_____

Make and Model:
_____

Owner:
_____

Location of Title:
_____

Owner:
_____

Location of title, title search, insurance, bill of sale, etc.:
_____

Outstanding Loan Amount:
_____

Lender: _____

Address: _____

City, State, Zip: _____

Phone: _____

Other Assets

Boats, RVs, farm machinery, manuscripts, furs, firearms, jewelry, objects d'art, and other assets whose existence, location, or value may not be immediately recognized. Describe each asset as fully as appropriate. Attach receipts if appropriate.

_____

_____

_____

_____

_____

I Want You to Know

*"Live as if you were to die tomorrow.
Learn as if you were to live forever."*

~~Mahatma Gandhi

I Want You to Know

Online Presence

Consider the challenge presented by your online presence after the time of your death. Who will manage your online banking, insurance policies, shopping sites, and all your social media hotspots? Every account and password should be documented in one place. If you are not comfortable with using this workbook for that information, write it all down and make sure that at least one person close to you knows where it is located. Then, be sure to keep it updated! Passwords should be updated frequently so be sure to keep your master list updated.

Facebook*

Name:
_____
User Name:
_____
Email:
_____
Password:
_____

* Facebook now allows you to appoint a legacy contact in the case of your death.

Twitter

Name:
_____
Username:
_____
Email:
_____
Password:
_____

I Want You to Know

Instagram

Name:
_____
User Name:
_____
Email:
_____
Password:
_____

Pinterest

Name:
_____
User Name:
_____
Email:
_____
Password:
_____

LinkedIn

Name:
_____
User Name:
_____
Email:
_____
Password:
_____

I Want You to Know

Google +

Name:
_____

User Name:
_____

Email:
_____

Password:
_____

Snapchat

Name:
_____

User Name:
_____

Email:
_____

Password:
_____

Tumblr

Name:
_____

User Name:
_____

Email:
_____

Password:
_____

YouTube

Name:
_____
User Name:
_____
Email:
_____
Password:
_____

Vine

Name:
_____
User Name:
_____
Email:
_____
Password:
_____

Site Name:

_____
Name:
_____
User Name:
_____
Email:
_____
Password:
_____

I Want You to Know

Site Name:
_____

Name:
_____

User Name:
_____

Email:
_____

Password:
_____

Site Name:
_____

Name:
_____

User Name:
_____

Email:
_____

Password:
_____

"There are only two mistakes one can make along the road to truth; not going all the way, and not starting."

~~Buddha

I Want You to Know

Power of Attorney, Advance Directives and Wills

Unless you are an attorney or perhaps a paralegal, this chapter may just make your eyes glaze over. Alas, it is important stuff to both understand and document, so bear with me. Soon we'll be moving on to the really exciting stuff. Yes, I said exciting! It's exciting because you will know yourself so much better by the time you are done. You will have a deeper understanding of what is truly important to you; in fact, you may just want to send me a thank you note when you are all finished!

The lasting legacy of Terri Schiavo has been an ever increasing number of our population that want a way to effectively take the burden of decision making off the shoulders of those they love. As you probably remember, Terri Schiavo, a St. Petersburg, Florida resident had been in a prolonged vegetative state due to causes still unknown that led her to collapse in her home at the age of 26. The subsequent oxygen deprivation after her collapse was the cause of her vegetative state. Ms. Schiavo had no living will. Therefore, all decisions as to what she would have wanted were in the hands of her husband and her parents. When Mr. Schiavo requested her feeding tube be removed in 1998, her parents immediately protested, launching both sides into a lengthy legal battle. It is high profile cases such as this that nullify the argument that young people do not need plans in place in case they should suffer either a life changing illness or injury. The final chapter in the Schiavo story is one of heartbreak for each of the human lives affected.

Surely it is not anyone's desire to leave the heavy burden of medical decisions to their family members. We procrastinate, we stick our heads in the sand, we believe in the best and hopefully we won't be caught short. Isn't it better to take what is basically a very short amount of time to commit your wishes to paper? Do you see how this is an act of love in action for those you hold dear?

What is a Power of Attorney?

A power of attorney is a document in which the principal (you) gives another person (agent or attorney-in-fact) legal authority to act on your behalf, typically in regard to financial and business matters. It can be granted to take effect immediately, or just in special circumstances; it can restrict the things the agent can do and/or the amount of money spent.

Even someone over the age of 18 may desire a power of attorney. Military personnel may designate a POA before being deployed overseas. A person who travels a great deal may appoint someone to act on their behalf, especially if they don't have a spouse to speak for them if they are not able.

How does a Power of Attorney work?

You choose someone that you trust to handle your affairs in your best interest should you have an emergency. It is important to note here that your spouse does not automatically have your power of attorney over any property that is only in your name. This is a just one example of the importance of having someone designated should something happen to you. You can designate how you want your POA set up. Perhaps you only want it to kick in if you are no longer capable of handling your affairs yourself, or you may want a power of attorney that automatically goes into effect immediately so the agent you appoint would be able to make decisions on your behalf right away in an emergency.

Why is a POA important?

This document may become the very instrument that protects your financial and property interests, your health, and even the manner in which you may die. Think about this for a moment: if you suddenly become incapacitated and you have not designated a POA to take over, your loved ones will probably be forced into costly and time-consuming delays while everything is sorted out. A POA is for your benefit, your peace of mind, but even more than that, it is going to assure that your best interests are immediately and legally being recognized.

You have to set this document up for yourself. A family can't just suddenly "get" a power of attorney when they have a realization that you've stroked out and will never regain all your mental abilities. The court can appoint a guardian or a conservator and no one has any control over who it is that is appointed.

When there is no power of attorney in some states, the guardian may have to post a bond and then they are required to file a complete inventory and accounting of the person's assets. I know this sounds complicated, and it is. It also strips away all your privacy. That power of attorney is sounding a lot better to you now, isn't it?

Each state has different requirements for a POA and there is no uniform law governing them. Don't make the mistake of thinking that a POA can be a substitute for a will. Wills are designed to designate who gets what after the event of your death. A power of attorney supports the continued critical financial and/or medically related decisions that you need to have made if you cannot make them yourself.

What are the different types of Power of Attorney?

Conventional

Conventional power of attorney starts as soon as it is signed and then continues until you become mentally unable to make sound decisions. In a conventional power of attorney, you need to state exactly what authority you are giving to the person you appoint as your agent. The most frequent use is what is known as a limited power of attorney. Perhaps you are not able to be present for the closing on the sale of a property and you appoint your attorney to have the authority to sign the deed of sale. In contrast, you could appoint another person to have much broader powers in your financial matters such as access to all your bank accounts, if that is what is needed.

Durable

The durable power of attorney also starts as soon as it is signed, but it lasts until your death, unless you specifically cancel it. Download a form for the state you reside in, fill it in with the representative present to assure you are both in agreement with the terms, and authorize it in front of a Notary Public. (Notaries are available at all banks)

I have a

____ Conventional Power of Attorney
____ Durable Power of Attorney

It/They can be found _____ Attached to these pages

I Want You to Know

Or located here:

I have a copy filed with:

_____

Advance Directives

This is where things can become exceedingly confusing. First and foremost, after reading what is written here, do an online search for ALL the forms required for your state of residence and follow only what they require. Anything written here is for general knowledge only, and to help you understand what the different types of forms are. Under the heading of advance directives come many forms. Heath care power of attorney, health care proxy, MOLST, POLST, DNR, living will, 5 Wishes. Some are recognized in some states, but not in others.

The health care power of attorney (medical power of attorney) is a document that designates someone to be your representative (agent) in the event you can no longer make or communicate your wishes about any aspect of your health care. Basically, you are saying, "I want this person to make all decisions about my health care if I cannot".

This is a very important decision so take the time needed to really think through who you would entrust with this responsibility. Many times people immediately assume they want it to be their spouse. Upon closer examination, you may realize that it should be someone else. Do you want to burden your spouse with the responsibility to make decisions that they may not agree with? If your spouse is adamantly opposed to removing life support, do you want them to have to carry out that decision for you if you have indicated you will want life support removed under certain circumstances? Whomever you choose, be sure they have the inner strength and fortitude to uphold your wishes, morals, and religious beliefs no matter what.

A health care power of attorney goes beyond a living will. A living will applies only if you are terminally ill or permanently unconscious or some other similar condition that has been defined by your state's law. For example, if you are unconscious but only temporarily so, a living will is of no use to your circumstances. This is the type of circumstance where you need a health care power of attorney.

It is possible to combine a living will and a health care power of attorney in one document. Research your state's options. A health care power of attorney can reach as broadly as you wish, or can limit the types of decisions the agent can make. Many people want to have a separate living will that gives your designated agent some guidance, or they put some living will provision into their healthcare power of attorney.

What are MOLST, POLST, health care proxy, and living will forms, and are they are basically the same thing? A health care proxy is a legal document in which the principal (you) appoint an agent to make your health care decisions for you. This agent will only have the authority to make medical decisions when a doctor certifies that you cannot make or communicate your own decisions. In the states in which it is recognized, it continues to be the only legal document which is binding on medical professionals. The heath care proxy must be signed by you and two neutral witnesses.

MOLST (medical orders for life sustaining treatment) or POLST (physician's orders for life sustaining treatment) is a document giving medical orders about life-sustaining treatment for patients with an already advanced illness. These forms are not used for those that are still healthy. How are a MOLST form and a health care proxy different? A health care proxy is for everyone, no matter the state of your health. You will notice in the health care proxy that there is no language about end-of-life-treatment. Its purpose is to appoint a heath care agent. In the MOLST, there are decisions concerning both emergency treatment and end-of-life concerns specific to the patient's illness. The wishes you document in your MOLST or POLST can be honored by EMTs and by emergency room personnel.

Living wills are a written statement detailing a person's desires regarding their medical treatment in circumstances in which they are no longer able to express informed consent, especially an advance directive.

DNR is a form stating that you choose to not be resuscitated should your heart cease to function. Again, each state has different requirements, so you must research what is required for your state of residence. In the State of

Massachusetts, for example, you can obtain at your request a DNR for use inside of a hospital which must be signed by your doctor. Outside the

I Want You to Know

hospital, you must complete a Massachusetts DNR form that will alert paramedics who would respond to any emergency at home, at a restaurant, etc. You must also obtain a MedicAlert or other bracelet, anklet, or necklace to make your wishes obvious to emergency medical personnel. This form also needs to be signed by a doctor or other approved medical professional.

"Five Wishes"

A very popular format for a living will is Five Wishes. Five Wishes is used in all 50 states and in countries around the world. It meets the legal requirements for an advance directive in 42 states and the District of Columbia. In the other eight states, your completed Five Wishes can be attached to your state's required form.

Five Wishes was started after Jim Towey worked with Mother Teresa and spent a year living in a hospice she ran in Washington, DC. He wanted a way for patients and their families to be able to plan ahead and better cope with serious illnesses. The form can be found by a google search. Once filled out it needs to be signed and notarized to become a legal document.

I have a _____ Health care Power of Attorney

_____ Living Will

_____ 5 Wishes

_____ DNR (outside of hospital)

_____ Health Care Proxy

_____ MOLST/POLST

It/They can be found _____ Attached to these pages
Or located here:
_____
I have a copy filed with:
_____

Wills

Wills get ignored and put off for so many reasons. As silly as it sounds, many people don't write a will because they view it as the ultimate sign of letting go of their youth. You are admitting that, in fact, you are an adult when you write a will. The unexpected death of Prince in April 2016 was shocking, as was finding out that he did not have a will. He's in rich company. Here are a few other people that may surprise you to learn never wrote a will.

Abraham Lincoln, Barry White, Martin Luther King Jr., Jimi Hendrix, and Pablo Picasso are just a few rather famous people that never penned their last will and testament.

Sadly, the result of NOT having a will could be that your loved ones may not receive the very assets that you wish them to have in the event of your death. Contrary to popular belief, wills do not need to be complicated, nor does it need to be expensive to have a will drawn up. A very basic will that can be completed online through Legal Zoom starts at $69 at the time of writing of this workbook in 2016. It can take as little as 15 minutes to complete!

What exactly is a will? A will is a legal document that sets forward your wishes regarding the distribution of your property and the care of any minor children. You want a will that is in writing and is signed by you and your witnesses. If you do not follow those steps, your instructions may not be carried out.

Really anyone that has any assets should have a will to allow you to have sole discretion over the distribution of those assets. A will directs how your belongings (cars, heirlooms, artwork, etc.) should be distributed. If you have your own business or investments, your will can make the transition of those assets a smooth event.

Anyone with minor children must provide for their care through the drafting of a will. The future of your children and the home in which they are raised is not something you want the state to decide on their behalf. Even if your children from another marriage are of adult age, you can assign the assets they receive upon your death.

I Want You to Know

There are inevitable tensions over assets among family members after a death, but tensions are greatly reduced with a clear will and assigning of your earthly possessions. You can also name charities, institutions, or other organizations to be the beneficiary of your assets.

Did you know that there are certain things your will does not cover? The proceeds from your life insurance policy payouts, your retirement assets, any investment that is designated as transfer on death, community property, and any assets that are owned as joint tenants with right of survivorship are not covered through your last will and testament.

There are different types of wills. We will outline them all here because they are not all recognized.

Self-Proving/Testamentary Will

This is the traditional will that most of us are familiar with. It is a document that states your wishes in the event of your death and outlines care of any minor children. This type of will is signed in the presence of witnesses. The original should be kept with you in the event that you move.

Your attorney will keep a copy and some people also choose to have at least one other person retain a copy.

Oral Will

This type of will is a spoken or oral testament that is given in front of witnesses. Rarely are these recognized as a legal and binding document.

Holographic Will

These wills are written without the presence of witnesses and they are not filed with an attorney. They are rarely held up in a court of law.

Living Will

These wills have nothing to do with the distribution of assets. They set forth your wishes for medical care in terms of life support should you become incapacitated permanently.

Scared Straight

It's easy to procrastinate making a will. When you are younger, you think you will live forever. When you start having children, you are busy and distracted, and it is easy to procrastinate. When you reach middle age, you start to feel guilty that you never made and filed a will. We don't like to feel guilty so it becomes easy to procrastinate. Then sometimes, fate intervenes and we get caught without a will, and suddenly, it is too late.

When you die with no will, the term is called intestate (meaning, one who had died with no will in place). What that means exactly is that the State of your residence upon your death will have control over the distribution of all your assets. Each state has a formula in place for this purpose.

For the sake of illustration, if you should die with no will with a surviving spouse and two children, normally the state would leave half of your estate to your spouse and half to your children. Keep in mind, this distribution means all assets, which of course could mean the family home, and any secondary property such as a vacation home. This could certainly make life even sadder in the aftermath of your death. Homes and other assets may need to be sold to equally divide the value of the assets, and it very well may make things much more difficult for the financial well-being of your surviving spouse.

Adjusting to life after the death of a spouse is difficult enough. Imagine the effect of losing half of what you thought you would have for assets to support the life style you have been living.

If that weren't upsetting enough, just think about the far reaching effects of the state appointing a representative of their choosing to oversee the financial interests of your minor children, should there be no will to disclose your wishes for the disbursement of your estate.

If there is no living parent after your death, the state will also oversee what happens to the upbringing of your children. I can only speak for myself when I say how much I would never want that to be the case for the sake of my children.

One last issue to think about regarding your estate without a will would be taxation. Utilizing the advice of an estate attorney can result in the crafting

I Want You to Know

of a will that minimizes tax liability for your benefactors. The larger the estate, the more important that becomes.

Will Facts

Before meeting with an attorney or going online to use an online portal such as Legal Zoom, make a thorough list of all your assets and all your debts. Don't forget about sentimental items, heirlooms, and what is inside your safety deposit box. The larger your estate, the more complicated your will needs to be so be sure to retain an attorney who is well versed in your state's laws and will composition. For many people, the software programs available online and web based programs can easily take care of your will requirements. Their instructions are usually easy to follow. You can be general in the wording you choose, (ex. I give my entire estate to my husband), or you can be very specific in nature. (ex. I give my diamond ring to my youngest daughter Nancy.) Clearly, the more specific you are, the better for those that are left behind to sort through your estate. Should you need to change your will down the road, you will just want to create an entirely new will, or make an addition called a codicil. Of course, the ideal is that we all create our wills when we are still of sound mind and body. This keeps heirs from being able to challenge changes you may have made.

Once you have completed your will, and it has been signed and witnessed, you will keep the original for yourself. If you move out of state or out of the region, you will still have your original with you. A copy will be kept with your attorney, and a copy will be kept with the person you have appointed to be the executor of your will.

Writing your will sounds and feels like such a huge ordeal. The great thing is that once you have written down your assets, the rest is really quite easy. It's the first big step in creating your legacy and creating your legacy is love in action.

I read a poignant letter written by the witness to a hit and run accident in San Francisco. A 26-year-old woman was riding her bike safely when an SUV sped through a red light, hit the woman and sped away. Although she was resuscitated at the scene, she succumbed to her injuries at the hospital a short while later. In our 20's and 30's we tend to still think of ourselves as invincible. Sadly, we are not and many times do not reach an old age. Pre-planning is imperative for all of us.

I Want You to Know

It is interesting that even as we age into our 40's and 50's, we may still have that, "I'm going to live forever" mindset. Even when we acknowledge that we aren't going to live forever, our human nature tends to lull us into a belief that we will always have enough time to set our affairs in order before it is needed.

More than any other adult task, wills are the easiest to procrastinate. The story that follows below helps illustrate why, no matter what your age, once you are an adult you should have a signed and notarized will in place. No one knows the time of their death.

Ivy had been divorced from her husband for several years when he died unexpectedly. With one child living close by and another across the country, she was asked to help her son in the final preparations for her ex-husband. Not only did her ex leave no will, he also had no life insurance, nor did he have any instructions for his disposition. Things became troublesome quickly when her ex-husband's family responded to their inner distress of adjusting to the shock of the sudden death. Complicating their emotions was a good deal of residual anger and resentment toward Ivy from the divorce. After all, who did Ivy think she was to voice her opinions on what David would have wanted? She is the one that left the marriage after all. Why should she be given any say now? The lack of a life insurance policy opened up more wounds as fragile discussions needed to be held while everyone was already at the peak of raw emotions.

Who would pay for David's funeral? The word quickly spread through the small Midwestern town David had lived in for several decades that the family was in a state of implosion. Soon a fund was started, and not long after, there was enough to pay for a small, no frills funeral and burial. Even though the estate was very small, it took several years to settle, and through that process, even more relationships within the family were permanently severed.

The financial and inter-personal strain was only part of what the family experienced. Imagine entering the home of someone who had passed unexpectedly and finding the half glass of red wine left from their early evening ritual and an open book on the table next to their chair. You pick up the book to the open pages and begin reading, wondering, what was the last line they read before they died? These things are what hold us spell bound in a state of disbelief. It takes time to claw our way through the cotton batting of denial to even get to the other side which holds still more disbelief and sadness and loss.

These are the experiences every human being should be able to sit with and journey through. To add to this with the pragmatic decisions required when no instructions are left; no plan, and no will is truly a cruel and unusual punishment.

~~~~~~

___ I have a will and it can be found

___ Attached to these pages

___ in this location:

___ In the possession of my:

___ Attorney:

Address:

_____

City, State, Zip:

_____

Phone:

_____

___ Executor:

Address:

_____

City, State, Zip:

_____

Phone:

_____

I Want You to Know

____ Spouse/Partner/Other:

Address:
_____

City, State, Zip:
_____

Phone:
_____

____ Child/Other:

Address:
_____

City, State, Zip:
_____

Phone:
_____

Designated Agent for Body Disposition:

The designated agent form allows you to name an individual to be in charge of the disposition of your body and any funeral or memorial arrangements. This can be especially helpful if there is any chance that your survivors will not agree on the disposition of your body (cremation, donation, etc.), funeral wishes (ex. religious service), and if your survivors are interested in family led death care or to make as many arrangements as possible without using a funeral director. Not every state has a designated agent for body disposition form. Check funerals.org/forconsumersmenu, select "Your Legal Rights", and then "Who Has the Right to Make Decisions About Your Funeral?"

PLEASE REMEMBER: THIS IS NOT A LEGAL DOCUMENT

I have a Designated Agent Form and it can be found:

_____ Attached to these pages
_____ In this location:
_____

_____ In the possession of my:
_____

I Want You to Know

_____ Designated Agent

Name:
_____

Relationship:
_____

Address:
_____

City, State, Zip:
_____

Phone:
_____

_____ Alternate Agent

Name:
_____

Relationship:
_____

Address:
_____

City, State, Zip:
_____

Phone:
_____

Pre need Arrangement Details

Pre need agreement with:
_____

Funeral Home/other:
_____

Address:
_____

Phone:
_____

I Want You to Know

Contact number and location:

_____

_____

I am a member of a cremation/funeral/memorial society:

Name:
_____
City, State, Zip:
_____
Phone:
_____
Contract number and location:
_____

Final disposition arrangements:

Town:
_____

Burial Plot: _____ Crypt: _____ Mausoleum: _____

Niche: _____ Vault: _____

Name:
_____
Location:
_____
Phone:
_____
Contract:
_____

Insurance Policy to cover final disposition:

Company Name:
_____

Agent's Name:
_____

Phone:
_____

Policy Number:
_____

Policy Location:
_____

Funeral Trust Account pay on death account:

Bank Name:
_____

Phone:
_____

Address:
_____

Account Number:
_____

Joint Account Holder Name:
_____

Amount:
_____

I Want You to Know

*"An animal's eyes have the power to
speak a great language."*

~~ Martin Buber

Beloved Pets

When Dorothy's ex-husband, Brad, died unexpectedly, he left behind a middle aged dog and cat. Because Brad lived alone and was a private person, almost a week passed before anyone came to the house to check on his whereabouts. The actions of Brad's dog Max, when someone finally appeared on the porch, told the tale that something was deeply amiss inside the home. The strain of being left alone for almost a week left deep dark impressions on both pets that resulted in a quiet desperate depression in his cat, Buster. But in his dog, it resulted in cowering on the couch cushions during the day, followed by spells of nocturnal bellowing as Max tried to secure his place in strange new surroundings without his beloved person.

Max and Buster were fortunate because Brad's daughter felt a deep sense of responsibility for their care. She made sure that not only were great homes provided, but they went to live in apartments in the same building.

Fortunately, both recovered with love and tender care from their new families, so this story does end happily for these four legged friends, but not so for many others.

The terrorist attacks of 9/11 left behind approximately 800 pets orphaned when their owners perished. 800 pets whose person never returned home that night to fill their water bowls, scratch their ears, and cuddle with them on the couch. Many of them sat in the dark, hungry and needing a walk. Sadly, one of the last things to be considered when planning for our eventual death is what will happen to our pets who depend on us for everything. We mistakenly think that we will outlive our animals because their life expectancy is so much shorter than our own. However, all too often after an unexpected death, the care of animals has not been taken into consideration and they are suddenly left uncared for.

Dorothy was profoundly affected by every aspect of her former husband's death, but the trauma of what she witnessed with the animals that were left behind prompted her to re-write her will to include a section pertaining to her own pets*. As both her pets are now aging, she knows they will probably not outlive her and she expects she'll never desire to have another at her age. She simply doesn't want history to be repeated, which may put her daughter once again in a difficult and stressful situation. She told me *that this experience brought a deeper relationship with her own pets to the extent that she spends more time engaged with them than before the loss of her ex-husband. She sees things through their eyes now and cares about how her actions impact their journey on this earth. Her feelings of companionship have more depth and meaning now. You've heard me use the term pre-planning is love in action, and now we see how a sad and heartbreaking situation prompted Dorothy to emanate love in action with her own pets.*

*Something important to take into consideration is the validity of adding pet care into a will. It seems to make sense at the outset, but realize that a will only takes effect upon death, and is not probated or formally recognized by the court for days or even weeks. If any legal dispute arises, the final settlement may be prolonged. It may, in fact, take a long time before your instructions regarding your pet's long-term care could be carried out.

A trust set up for your pet(s) could provide for immediate care. It also can be used if you become seriously ill or incapacitated as it does not need to wait until your death. You are the one that can determine when the trust you set up goes into effect. At the same time, you set up a trust, you can set aside money to be used for pet care, and specify the trustee to control those funds.

Here we have an opportunity to spend some time thinking about what is best for our animals should something happen to us. As in the rest of this guide, the section on pet care is not meant to be substituted in any way for legal advice. The following pages are mean to serve as supplementary ideas and suggestions for consideration. Please employ the services of an attorney for all legal documentation.

Your attorney can help advise you on what type of document best suits your particular needs. There are many considerations to weigh, and the legal advice of your attorney will help sort through what is best for your situation. Each state has different requirements that need to be upheld. Also, remember that tying up substantial amounts of money or property in a trust for an animal's benefit could be seen as controversial for your heirs. Trusts can be relatively expensive to maintain and difficult to administer so it is important to have careful planning and solid legal counseling. Be sure to leave a copy of the trust and/or will with the designated caregiver so your pet will be cared for immediately upon death or serious illness or injury. Of course, the executor and the caregiver may not be the same person, so be sure to have all important parties given the paperwork they need. You will also want to make sure that the caregiver has all your pet's veterinarian records and information about their dietary needs, desires, and behavior traits.

Power of Attorney

As you prepare your general power of attorney, you can also authorize your designee to take care of your pets or even place your pets with permanent caregivers if appropriate for your circumstances. Providing care instructions in this way is simpler than a trust and also does not create a legal entity that needs to be maintained by formal means. You can determine the POA to take effect if you are physically or mentally incapacitated and continue in effect afterward. Your attorney can help you decide if this is the best choice for you.

Remember that no legal device can ensure that your pet is fed, medicated as needed, walked, and cared for daily. Legal devices are meant to only complement your personal efforts to be organized and think ahead to find temporary or permanent homes for your beloved pets.

Choosing Caregivers

Will you want all of your pets to go to one caregiver, or have individual pets go to different caregivers? The best answers are based completely on your unique circumstances. Clearly the care of a large pet snake is vastly different than that of a Chihuahua. The same person may not be the best choice for those two pets to be placed together. If you have pets that have bonded relationships, it would be best for them to stay together when possible. Whoever your choice is, be sure to have an alternative in place for each pet in case your first caregiver choice is suddenly not available.

Have detailed discussions with any potential caregivers so they understand everything they are agreeing to in the care of your pet. This should be someone you trust implicitly as they will have full say over every aspect of your pet's life.

Update, update, update! Just as you have been encouraged to review this entire document yearly, you will want to do the same with pet care choices. Other people's circumstances and priorities change and potential caregivers may move or undergo other life changes that make them no longer appropriate

I Want You to Know

or available to take on the care of your pet. Once a year, get in touch with both your first and the alternate caregiver candidate to confirm that they are still the best choice for your pet.

A helpful resource to read is *Fat Cats and Lucky Dogs*, by Barry Seltzer, Gerry Beyer, and Jim Bee. It provides valuable information to anyone with pets to ensure they provide properly for their pets long before an emergency arises.

Name your pets and who you have named to care for them should you not be able to.

Pet's Name:
_____

Designee for Care:
_____

Address:
_____

Phone:
_____

Pet's Name:
_____

Designee for Care:
_____

Address:
_____

Phone:
_____

Pet's Name:
_____

Designee for Care:
_____

Address:
_____

Phone:
_____

I Want You to Know

    Pet's Name:
_____
Designee for Care:
_____
Address:
_____
Phone:
_____

_____ I have a will that names information regarding my pet(s) care

A copy can be found here: _____

_____ I have power of attorney naming information regarding my pet(s) care

A copy can be found here: _____

_____ I have a trust that names information regarding my pet(s) care

A copy can be found here: _____

    Prepare an entire packet of information on each pet including their veterinarian information, their vaccination history, allergies, food needs, and any special requirements. In addition, be sure to include information on their personalities and preferences. Do they love to go for long walks? Hate the rain? Love riding on boats? Mostly sedentary? Love kids? Hate other dogs? All aspects of what makes them unique should be in their "person packet". A copy of the packet should be included with this workbook, with the person you want to care for your pet and one for the alternate choice.

I Want You to Know

Following are suggestions for your packet, but feel free to add any information that is important in the care of your particular pet.

Pet Name: _____

Veterinarian: _____

Address: _____

Phone: _____

Vaccination: _____ Date: _____

Vaccination: _____ Date: _____

Vaccination: _____ Date: _____

Vaccination: _____ Date: _____

Vaccination: _____ Date: _____

Vaccination: _____ Date: _____

Allergies:
_____
_____
_____

Medications:
_____
_____
_____
_____

I Want You to Know

Dog Walker: _____

Address: _____

Phone: _____

Boarding Kennel: _____

Address: _____

Phone: _____

Trainer: _____

Address: _____

Phone: _____

Daily Food Regiment:

_____

_____

_____

_____

Special Requirements:

_____

_____

_____

_____

_____

I Want You to Know

Favorite Treats:
_____

Favorite Pastime:
_____

Sleep Regiment:
_____

What calms him/her:
_____

Personality:

_____

_____

_____

_____

_____

I Want You to Know

"I care not for a man's religion whose dog and cat are not the better for it."

~~Abraham Lincoln

I Want You to Know

Gifts

The law generally distinguishes between items that have intrinsic value and sentimental value. While your will is intended to settle the bulk of your estate, you may still have some personal belongings that you would like to leave to special people in your life. You may choose to include stories about your individual items to explain their significance to you, which will enhance their value to your loved one. Be sure to include the location of each item. Consult with your attorney regarding the best way to share the information of gift disbursement. This list is for your referral. As in the other segments of this workbook, this is not meant to be a legal document.

The following items may be removed by the person I have designated to receive them at any time:

Awards:
_____

Bible:
_____

Clothing:
_____

Letters:
_____

Photographs:
_____

These items need to be given and received prior to death or they become subject to probate:

_____Antique	_____Equipment
_____Artwork	_____Furniture
_____Books	_____Jewelry
_____Cars	_____Military Regalia
_____Collections	_____Pets*
_____Electronics	_____Plants

_____Rugs   _____Silver/China/Crystal

_____Tools   _____Wedding Gifts

_____Other   _____Other

Many people choose to gift their sentimental items while they are still alive. This can provide the opportunity for rich conversation, storytelling, passing on of family values, and generational history. Writing stories down is a way to capture family stories for generations to come.

Please refer to the chapter on pets.

I Want You to Know

"Fear does not stop death it stops life"

~~Unknown

End of Life Care

Is there another generation as vastly diverse as the baby boomer generation? While the "boomers" were born into a time of greater wealth and comfort than their parents, they grew into a splintering of value systems. The baby boomer generation is mostly known for their self-indulgence, debt and living beyond their means. But they are also the generation that refused to accept the status quo when they began to have children. Natural child-birth, home-schooling, walking out of standardized religion in droves, and setting a new course for finding their spiritual path on their own terms are all by-products of the baby boomer generation. As this group started to age to retirement and beyond, the family based after death care movement began to gain momentum, and people also began to embrace what they viewed as a "better death". They've re-written every other stage of the life cycle, why would this generation not be re-writing death care as well?

While it is true that the vast majority still shy away from conversations about their own death, there are many who are stepping up and becoming empowered about impacting their death journey. We cannot always know how we will die. We've seen that fact in its many faces as we have journeyed through this book. But what about when we have the time to know we are nearing death? 90% of us will know at least some time in advance that we are facing our end on this earth. We have a choice. We can use time we may be given to plan out our wishes for our end of life, or we can take that same amount of time and squander it on ignoring where we are and where we are headed. It is my goal that you will choose to not expend that time and energy on denial, but instead turn it into pre-planning and create your own legacy. I've heard a number of testimonials that people feel their most alive once they have created their will, assigned health care proxies, filed living wills and created a thorough death plan. It makes sense doesn't it? We make things so much worse than they really are when we play the game of dismissing the truth and ignore the big decisions. Once they are done, we feel free, we feel empowered. We feel the surge of energy that comes from truly showing our love by removing the burden of leaving decisions to our family that should have been made by us. We become the hero of our own life story.

I invite you to become your own hero and spend some time in these next chapters listening to your inner voice, digging into your inner knowing and stepping into who you really are. It is the best side effect of planning. By the time you finish these next chapters, you will know yourself better than you ever have, no matter what your age.

Much like every other chapter you have already completed, it is important to remember that your wishes may change over time. I have known people who were deeply committed to a home death because they wanted to be surrounded by their own things, their family and felt the privacy of their own home would ease their journey. However, based on their particular illnesses as they neared their final months or weeks, they knew that their medical care was going to be particularly challenging for their family to manage. Even with hospice in the home, there would be a great deal of intimate and unpleasant daily care that would fall to the family. They found nearby hospice facilities and utilized the added medical staff and resources available in the hospice setting. You will find that there is an opportunity to bring in some of your cherished items to make the room feel more like your home setting. Just know that you have options, and you have the right to change your mind based on what is currently happening in your own circumstances.

Before you begin filling in the forms in this chapter, I recommend taking a few moments to become fully present. Rushing through this work just to have it completed rather misses the whole point. As we shift from the pragmatic to the more soul-centered work, we need to give our inner selves the time to settle into this deeper planning. If you have your own favorite breathing exercise to gain your center, feel free to employ it now. I am not offering a set meditation here for a reason. If meditation is not a part of your normal life routine, it may feel off-putting to you. It may have the opposite effect of what I am hoping will be a slowing down and an intentional approach. If you are a user of meditation, you probably have your favorite method anyway. Should you be interested in learning a powerful and transformative meditation method, please do an internet search for either "metta" meditation or "loving kindness" meditation. Whatever your religious belief system, this particular meditation is truly approachable, easy, and I feel confident you'll love it. The result is a feeling of expansiveness and a greater love for yourself, those closest to you, and on and on. Who couldn't use a little more of those kinds of feelings? A beautiful by-product of this particular meditation is the benefit to the universe as all those loving thoughts and energies are spread ever wider out in the world.

I Want You to Know

For now, either use your favorite breathing method, short meditation, prayer, or just spend a few moments centering your intentions to becoming focused on what brings you comfort.

Spend some time thinking about the things you would want to have around you during your last days. It may be spiritual items, books, family mementos, or items from nature. I've had people tell me that they have no idea how they would choose just a few things because they have so many items that they love. I recommend this: envision building an altar*. If you were creating an altar for meditation that included only your most treasured items, what would it look like? From this experiment, you should be able to narrow down the list to the few things that really matter to you.

*Please, don't be put off by the term altar. I realize there will be some that might be aghast at the notion. We all build altars! Look at your desk, or bedside table. Are there photos of loved ones, or special places in your life? Do you find a gathering of perhaps a piece of driftwood from the shore, a beautiful stone from the forest, a favorite gemstone or a feather? That is an altar! A focal point for you of what is deeply personal and grounding. Isn't that concept beautiful?

Items of importance I will want around my bedside:

What things will bring you peace, calmness, joy, and inspiration during your final journey?

Music:
_____
Poetry/Other Reading:
_____
Touch/Massage/Reiki:
_____
Aromas:
_____
Essential Oils:
_____
Flowers:
_____

Natural Lighting:
_____

Window:
_____

Position of bed:
_____

Other requests not listed here:

_____

_____

_____

_____

There may be people that you can immediately see in your mind's eye as you think about your final days. If you spend a few moments thinking not only about your physical family, but your spiritual family and closest people, others may come to mind. It may be that your physical family wouldn't know who all those people are. List out all the names of those you would love by your bedside as you begin your death journey. Even the obvious names should be listed here.

When possible, I'd like the following people present at my death:

Name: _____ Phone: _____

Name: _____ Phone: _____

Name: _____ Phone: _____

Name: _____ Phone: _____

Name: _____ Phone: _____

Name: _____ Phone: _____

I Want You to Know

Name: _____ Phone: _____

Name: _____ Phone: _____

Name: _____ Phone: _____

Name: _____ Phone: _____

Name: _____ Phone: _____

Conversely, there may be people that you know with certainty that you would NOT want at your bedside if you were dying. This is not the time to be politically correct. This is your journey and you should not have to be stressed or anxious by someone showing up that you just don't want to be around. Frankly, it doesn't matter who it is. You have your own good reasons for how you feel. Don't hold back, list any names that you would not want present, for whatever reason. It could be because you know it would just be too hard on them or you. However, you feel, it is your decision and it is the right decision for you.

I do NOT want the following people present at my death vigil:

Name: _____ Phone: _____

Name: _____ Phone: _____

Name: _____ Phone: _____

Following death, I would like to have the following reading(s):

_____

_____

_____

_____

_____

I Want You to Know

Following death, I would like the following song(s) performed or sung:

_____

_____

_____

_____

_____

Following death, I would like to have a visit by a member of Clergy:

Name:
_____

Address:
_____

Phone:
_____

Following death, I would like to have a visit by a Celebrant:

Name:
_____

Address:
_____

Phone:
_____

Following death, I would like to have the following ritual performed:

_____

_____

_____

_____

_____

I Want You to Know

Included here is a notes section, as there may be things that you'd like to write in about this most important journey that have not been included in the information above:

_____

_____

_____

_____

_____

As a final note to this chapter, I wanted to include the Dying Person's Bill of Rights, created at a workshop entitled, "The Terminally Ill Patient and the Helping Person" in Lansing Michigan sponsored by the South Western Michigan Inservice Education Council and conducted by Amelia Barbux (1975), Associate Profession of Nursing, Wayne State University.

<u>Dying Person's Bill of Rights</u>

I have the right to be treated as a living human until I die.

I have the right to maintain a sense of hopefulness, however changing its focus may be.

I have the right to be cared for by those who can maintain a sense of hopefulness, however changing this may be.

I have the right to express my feelings and emotions about my approaching death in my own way.

I have the right to participate in decisions concerning my care.

I have the right to expect continuing medical and nursing attention even though "cure" goals must be changed to "comfort" goals.

I have the right to not die alone. I have the right to be free of pain.

I Want You to Know

I have the right to have my questions answered honestly.

I have the right to retain my individuality and not be judged for my decisions, which maybe contrary to the belief of others.

I have the right to expect that the sanctity of the human body will be respected after death.

I have the right to be cared for by caring, sensitive, knowledgeable people who will attempt to understand my needs and will be able to gain some satisfaction in helping me face my death.

I Want You to Know

"My life is my message."

~~Mahatma Gandhi

Information for After Death

You've done such important work throughout this book. You've gathered contact information, facts and figures. So far you have made things infinitely less stressful for your loved ones by your accomplishments.

To be sure your wishes are being realized, you'll want to name someone who is your point person to make things happen and make sure your wishes are carried out after your death. That starts with the gathering all your legal information after your death.

Gathering of Legal Information

I would like this task done by:
_____

Location of the following:
_____

Copy of will:
_____

Advanced directives concerning after death care:
_____

Pre-planned agreements with funeral home/crematory:

Title to burial plot:
_____

Birth certificate:
_____

Marriage certificate:
_____

Insurance policies:
_____

Bank records:
_____

Property deeds:
_____

Vehicle ownership records:
_____

Military discharge papers:
_____

Citizenship papers:
_____

Information for Obituary

Newspapers often have a prescribed format, but the following information is typically included. Many newspapers charge for obituaries to be published.

Date and place of death:
_____

Cause of death:
_____

Age at death: _____ City of residence: _____

Date of birth: _____ Place of birth: _____

Education and employment:
_____
_____
_____
_____
_____
_____

I Want You to Know

Religious, social, community, volunteer affiliations:

_____

_____

_____

_____

_____

_____

Hobbies, interests, honors, prizes, accomplishments:

_____

_____

_____

_____

_____

_____

_____

Children, close relatives (note that information about deceased relatives can be found in the basic information chapter

If there is a draft obituary, is it located: _____

Or, attached to these pages: _____

I Want You to Know

I would like my obituary to be placed in the following newspapers, alumni publications, etc.:

_____

_____

_____

_____

_____

_____

I would like to suggest memorial contributions be made to the following organizations:

Organization Name:
_____

Address:
_____

City, State, Zip:
_____

Phone: _____ Website: _____

Organization Name:
_____

Address:
_____

City, State, Zip:
_____

Phone: _____ Website: _____

I Want You to Know

Organization Name:
_____
Address:
_____
City, State, Zip:
_____
Phone: _____ Website: _____

There are many people that need to be notified after a death has happened. This can be an ongoing cause of stress to family members. There are so many people, organizations, affiliations and service providers that family members may not know. It makes the grieving process a lot more difficult to be receiving calls, questions, emails, and bills six months or even longer after a family member has died.

Let's look at all the people you will want to be notified upon your death.

We start with distant or distant family members that may not automatically have been contacted already.

Name: _____ Relationship: _____
Phone:
_____

Name: _____ Relationship: _____
Phone:
_____

Name: _____ Relationship: _____
Phone:
_____

Name: _____ Relationship: _____
Phone:
_____

Name: _____ Relationship: _____
Phone:
_____

I Want You to Know

Name: _____ Relationship: _____
Phone:
_____

Name: _____ Relationship: _____
Phone:
_____

Name: _____ Relationship: _____
Phone:
_____

Friends that you would like to have notified:

Name: _____ Relationship: _____
Phone:
_____

Name: _____ Relationship: _____
Phone:
_____

Name: _____ Relationship: _____
Phone:
_____

Name: _____ Relationship: _____
Phone:
_____

Name: _____ Relationship: _____
Phone:
_____

Name: _____ Relationship: _____
Phone:
_____

I Want You to Know

Name: _____ Relationship: _____
Phone:
_____

Name: _____ Relationship: _____
Phone:
_____

Neighbors that you would like to have notified:

Name: _____ Relationship: _____
Phone:
_____

Name: _____ Relationship: _____
Phone:
_____

Name: _____ Relationship: _____
Phone:
_____

Name: _____ Relationship: _____
Phone:
_____

Name: _____ Relationship: _____
Phone:
_____

Name: _____ Relationship: _____
Phone:
_____

Name: _____ Relationship: _____
Phone:
_____

I Want You to Know

Name: _____ Relationship: _____
Phone:
_____

Professional Providers that should be notified:

Employer:
_____

Phone:
_____

Physician:
_____

Phone:
_____

Physician:
_____

Phone:
_____

Physician:
_____

Phone:
_____

Physician:
_____

Phone:
_____

Physician:
_____

Phone:
_____

I Want You to Know

Dentist: _____

Phone: _____

Optometrist: _____

Phone: _____

Chiropractor: _____

Phone: _____

Acupuncturist: _____

Phone: _____

Massage: _____

Phone: _____

Pharmacy: _____

Phone: _____

Therapist: _____

Phone: _____

Other Healthcare Provider

Name:
_____

Phone:
_____

Other Healthcare Provider

Name:
_____

Phone:
_____

Attorney:
_____

Phone:
_____

Accountant:
_____

Phone:
_____

Financial Advisor:
_____

Phone:
_____

Professional Org:
_____

Phone:
_____

Professional Org:
_____

Phone:
_____

I Want You to Know

Religious/Spiritual/Clergy:
_____
Phone:
_____

Religious/Spiritual/Clergy:
_____
Phone:
_____

Yard/Garden Service:
_____
Phone:
_____

Pool Service:
_____
Phone:
_____

Snowplowing Service:
_____
Phone:
_____

Irrigation Service:
_____
Phone:
_____

Gutter Maintenance:
_____
Phone:
_____

Plumber:
_____
Phone:
_____

Electrician:
_____

Phone:
_____

HVAC:
_____

Phone:
_____

Generator Service:
_____

Phone:
_____

Chimney Service:
_____

Phone:
_____

Hair Salon:
_____

Phone:
_____

Note for family after a death has occurred:

Be sure to contact the Post Office immediately after a death has occurred. You don't want mail to start piling up! This is like taking out an advertisement that the home is unoccupied. You can easily file an address forwarding form to get started. This will help you keep track of magazine subscriptions you may not know about, and what other people may not have been notified of the death of your family member.

I Want You to Know

Utility Companies:

Gas:
_____

Phone:
_____

Account #:
_____

Electricity:
_____

Phone:
_____

Account #:
_____

Oil:
_____

Phone:
_____

Account #:
_____

Cable:
_____

Phone:
_____

Account #:
_____

Water:
_____

Phone:
_____

Account #:
_____

I Want You to Know

Internet:
_____

Phone:
_____

Account #:
_____

Phone Service:
_____

Phone:
_____

Account #:
_____

Mobile Phone Service:
_____

Phone:
_____

Account #:
_____

Other:
_____

Phone:
_____

Account #:
_____

Other:
_____

Phone:
_____

Account #:
_____

Veterinarian:
_____

Phone:
_____

I Want You to Know

Pet Sitter/Walker:
_____
Phone:
_____

Pet Boarding:
_____
Phone:
_____

Other:
_____
Phone:
_____

Other:
_____
Phone:
_____

Volunteer Services:

Organization: _____ Phone: _____

Organization: _____ Phone: _____

Organization: _____ Phone: _____

Clubs and Membership Organizations:

Health Club:
_____
Phone:
_____

Athletic Club:
_____
Phone:
_____

I Want You to Know

Professional Assoc.:
_____

Phone:
_____

Professional Assoc.:
_____

Phone:
_____

Union:
_____

Phone:
_____

Automobile Club:
_____

Phone:
_____

Golf Club Membership:
_____

Phone:
_____

Video Club:
_____

Phone:
_____

Netflix ID:
_____

Password:
_____

I Want You to Know

Type of Membership:

Hulu ID:
_____

Password:
_____

Type of Membership:

YouTube Paid:
_____

Password:
_____

Music Memberships

Spotify ID:
_____

Password:
_____

Type of Membership:

Pandora ID:
_____

Password:
_____

Type of Membership:

iTunes ID:
_____

Password:
_____

Audible Books:
_____

Password:
_____

I Want You to Know

Alumni Club:
_____

Phone:
_____

Public Library:
_____

Phone:
_____

Rotary Club:
_____

Phone:
_____

Kiwanis Club:
_____

Phone:
_____

Lions Club:
_____

Phone:
_____

Other Clubs and Organizations:

_____

_____

_____

_____

I Want You to Know

My address book can be located here for any other contacts that may not be listed in this section:

Government Agencies:

Social Security Administration _____ Phone 1-800-772-1213

Veteran's Admin. if you were in the military _____

Phone: _____

Defense Finance & Accounting Service for military service retiree Phone 800-269-5170

Office of Personnel Management if a federal civil service employee 1-888-767-6738
US Citizenship and Immigration Service if not a US Citizen 1-800-375-5283

State Department of Motor Vehicles

If you had a driver's license or State ID

Phone: _____

Financial Companies

Credit Card: _____ Phone: _____

Account #: _____

Online sign in ID: _____ Password: _____

Credit Card: _____ Phone: _____

Account #: _____

Online sign in ID: _____ Password: _____

Credit Card: _____ Phone: _____

I Want You to Know

Account #: _____

Online sign in ID: _____ Password: _____

Credit Card: _____ Phone: _____

Account #: _____

Online sign in ID: _____ Password: _____

Credit Card: _____ Phone: _____

Account #: _____

Online sign in ID: _____ Password: _____

Health, Medical, Dental, Disability, Automotive and Life Insurance Providers (contact information can be found in the Banking/Insurance Chapter)

Credit Reporting Agencies should be contacted after death. They should be instructed to list all accounts as "Closed. Account holder is deceased."

Should you desire, you can also request a credit report to obtain a list of all creditors and to review any recent credit card activities.

Experian Credit Reporting 1-888-397-3742

P.O. Box 9701 Allen, TX 75013

Equinox Credit Reporting 1-800-525-6285

P.O. Box 105069 Atlanta, GA 30348

TransUnion Credit Reporting 1-800-680-7289

P.O. Box 6790 Fullerton, CA 92834

Did you know you can place a deceased family member's name on the "Do Not Contact List"? For a small fee ($1.00 at the time of this book

I Want You to Know

publication) you can list the decedent's name on the "deceased do not contact list". This list is maintained by the direct marketing association. The members of the direct marketing association will delete the name from their mailing lists, once the name has been posted. At the time of publication, this is the website for registering the name: www.ims-dm.com/cgi/ddnc

The following will be required for the death certificate:

Social Security Number: _____

Sex: _____ Race: _____ Date of Birth: _____

Birthplace (city, state, country): _____

Armed Forces Services (war and dates):

_____

_____

_____

_____

_____

Marital Status: _____

Surviving Partner/Spouse Name (if wife, maiden name):

_____

Father's Name:
_____
Date of Birth:
_____
Mother's Maiden Name:
_____
Date of Birth:
_____

I Want You to Know

Highest Grade Completed/Degree:
_____

Occupation:
_____

I Want You to Know

"We're all just walking each other home"

~~Ram Dass

I Want You to Know

After Death Care and Family Led Death care

    This chapter, perhaps even more than the chapter on End of Life Care, is my love and passion. The quote at the beginning of this chapter is the simple reason why. Truly, we walk this plane together, and we all just walk each other home. At least, I believe strongly that is how it should be.

    Not so very many generations ago, caring for our own after death was the normal process. After a death, the neighborhood women gathered to bathe and dress the body while the men constructed a coffin, usually just a plain pine box. The body was laid out in the home and neighbors came to call, bearing food and drink, saying their final goodbyes and sharing stories of a life well lived.

    The tragic circumstances of the Civil War, with young men dying in battle hundreds of miles from home, started the barbaric process of embalming. The process happened right in the battlefields themselves. The bodies were then shipped home to be laid to rest on their family farms. When the war ended, the men who had the equipment and experience in embalming needed a way to continue making use of their talents and equipment. They set up shop in towns across the country initially offering embalming services and then continuing to expand into funeral services. The first funeral homes looked much like the home parlor, hence the name, Funeral Parlor. Little by little, we began to give away the ownership of caring for our own dead until it became the norm, not the exception.

    Fortunately, embalming has effectively fallen from favor with the American public, as we have become aware of the extreme toxicity of not only the process itself, but to our environment as those embalmed bodies decay and eventually return to the earth. Most people do not understand the process of embalming. If they did, it would have been shunned long ago. However, the idea of caring for your loved one at home was usually met with an aghast expression and a quick negative response. This, too, is beginning to shift as more and more people begin to understand the deeply healing benefits of caring for our loved ones at home.

    This subject could fill a book in itself, so we'll merely give an overview here. When you think about the cycle of life for any of us that were born anytime in the 50's and beyond, we have embraced the ownership of every part of life. We took on mainstream medicine and we've demanded more natural approaches to our medical care. We now care for our aging parents and terminal loved ones at home as much as we can to gift them with the intimacy and spiritual connection you can only get in a home setting. When needed, we bring in hospice and hire home health aides to assist in clinical care while we care for our loved one's hearts, minds, and souls. Why then, after they release their final breath, do we call a "professional" to whisk them away to be cared for by strangers?

Family led death care is the final frontier of embracing the ownership of our loved one's final disposition. There is a quickly expanding movement to empower family members to keep their dear ones in the home for at least a short time after death has occurred. The ritual of gathering a small group from the neighborhood or family members, removing now unnecessary medical equipment, bathing and dressing the body, and laying them out with special mementos is a deeply moving experience and allows a healthy flow of grief to begin. What a loving and gentle release this is for our dear family member.

There is something about being right in it and of being part of this final act of love and reverence that gives your grief somewhere to go. When asked, families who have participated in home funerals have very similar testimonials. It helps you realize that, in fact, your loved one is no longer there. The body is but a shell; their spirit has definitely departed.

From Max Alexander, Smithsonian Magazine 3-2009 by way of the National Home Funeral Alliance Website:

"He looked unquestionably dead, but he looked beautiful. Harper and I received many compliments on our coffin. Later, when the wine flowed and the kitchen rang with laughter and Bob was alone again, I went in to see him. I held his cool hands and remembered how, not so long ago, those hands were tying fishing lures, strumming a banjo, splitting wood. Those days were over, and that made me sad, but it also felt OK."

Though it may appear so from the beginning portion of this chapter, this section really is not just about the promoting of home funerals. I do want the readers of this book to be aware that the opportunity exists. There are organizations that can assist with education and support, such as the National Home Funeral Alliance. I also encourage people to look into the green burial movement to understand more about the toxic load of the standard American burial process. The facts will stagger you. Consider this: the funeral industry results in the harvesting of 30 million board feet of casket wood (some of which is tropical hardwoods), 90,000 tons of steel, 1.6 million tons of concrete (vaults), and 800,000 gallons of toxic embalming fluid annually. We're all adults here, right? I know we all realize that even with embalming and sealed caskets and liners that the human body does still decompose, as does everything. Those toxins are leeching out into our soils and into our already compromised water tables.

    The other important thing to consider as you think of the option of family lead death care after your death is that you can request that your family do as much or as little as feels appropriate. You may decide that you would like to have your family join together to bathe and dress your body in your favorite outfit and keep you at home over the first night with the funeral home arriving the next morning to take over the rest of the funeral or memorial process. This journey should not be full of rules or worrying that your family will feel guilty if they just can't take on the entire home funeral process. Consider the options, ask questions, and then request to have done what feels right for you and for your family. This is wonderful as a group and family discussion when possible.

    I offer up this story as a beautiful and poignant example of what a home funeral did for one woman who shared her story with me. I was so moved by her personal reflections on the experience of participating in a home funeral that I am including her words in their entirety with the only change being in the name of the participants.

*   My friend Serena died after being diagnosed with cancer. In her last years, she was very active in learning about and advocating for green burial options in her hometown, so her friends knew very well how she wanted to be buried. We knew it was coming; her decline was interspersed with some respite, but we still knew she would die. I felt helpless during her illness. I did not really know how I could help or what to do to make her feel better. I didn't visit much, only on a few occasions. When she passed and plans for her funeral were being put into action, I followed the preparations around her circle of friends and realized that the one thing I could really contribute was the transportation aspect: I drive a black minivan (with lots of bumper stickers). I occasionally feel guilty about driving such a gas guzzler, but in this situation, it was exactly what we needed.*

I Want You to Know

On the day of the funeral, I made sure to be there early and take measurements to make sure there were no last minute problems. We spoke with the local police officers about the traffic situation and route to take, how to proceed at busy intersections, etc. I felt a sense of responsibility, which was oddly helpful. At other funerals, I have felt out of place, not knowing what to do or what to say. Here, I felt such a sense of people appreciating each other, pulling together, each of us doing what we felt like we could to contribute.

Because I homeschool, I brought my 9-year-old daughter with me. I wondered how she would feel. She had known Serena and had been to the house before. The day of the funeral was different. We learned about Jewish funeral traditions and rites, and a friend, whom I knew only as a 'civilian' until then, was the Rabbi who performed the ceremony. We were all a bit squished in Serena's small, all-purpose living space - people reading poems, a song was played on a boom box that she had chosen, "Jump Mama" (we were all laughing and crying at the same time). At the end of the ceremony, Serena's friends and family carried the simple pine coffin, made by her friends, and decorated with crayons by those attending the funeral, out into my car.

The Rabbi was riding with me, and I will never forget that car ride. We both were in tears over the kindness of the police officers, who went above and beyond to make our journey a smooth one. I felt like I was able to give Serena what we Germans call the 'last company'. I could make one bit of this journey with her. We said to her in the car: "See what you have done? See what you have accomplished?" Hers was the first green burial and home funeral to take place in her hometown in recent history, due to her own advocacy.

The grave site was on the edge of a Jewish cemetery, looking out into the conservation land. I know she was very excited (and that was the word she used when she told me, prior to her cancer diagnosis, prompting me to look at her funny) to have her body return to the circle of life within our ecosystem. We learned of the Jewish tradition to stop several times on the way to the grave, to show how reluctantly we let go of our friend. More prayer, and then we all filled in the grave together, taking turns with several shovels. People offered songs to accompany the shoveling. When the grave was filled, I spoke to my friends, Serena's friends, in quiet voices. We all thought this last act of filling the grave with dirt while singing was perfect and so very

I Want You to Know

meaningful. My daughter and my friend's daughter of similar age had never known any other type of burial or funeral, and everything seemed perfectly natural to them. I thought how lucky that their first encounter with death and burial was such an intentional and personal one.

We returned to the house, but didn't stay long, wanting to leave the family to spend their time together.

*Serena's wish to have a home funeral has, in the end, brought her friends closer together, and it has given me a much more positive outlook on burial. I told my friend, who was one of Serena's closest friends and number one ally in the quest to learn about home funerals and green burial, that she will be in my will to plan mine one day. * She accepted, I am lucky. When I go back to that day in my mind, I recall the car ride and the act of filling the grave as two of the most meaningful moments to me. I know that others have had their own moments that really stayed with them. My friend told me how she and Serena's daughter washed and shrouded her, bonding and connecting in the process. Others may have contributed with their own talents such as woodworking or singing. Even the Rabbi, who had done many funerals, found this one profound and moving. We all spoke about our experience in a gathering a few weeks later - and none of us have come away unchanged.*

*Please keep in mind that a will is not the optimum form to name someone as your designee to plan your home based funeral as wills are not normally read until after a final disposition. Please refer to the area below to designate a point person to oversee your family led funeral/memorial wishes.

___ I would like to have family led death care after I die.

___ I would like my family to bathe and dress me and then call the funeral home.

___ I would like my family to bathe and dress me, then lay out my body for visitation. I would like to be kept at home for: _____.

___ I am not interested in any family led death care after my death and prefer to have the funeral home called when my family is ready.

I Want You to Know

Should you desire family led death care you can designate more of your wishes below.

Person I would like to designate to oversee my family led funeral/memorial:

Name: _____

Address: _____

Phone: _____

People I would like to serve as personal care attendants after my death:

Name: _____ Phone: _____

Email: _____

Name: _____ Phone: _____

Email: _____

Name: _____ Phone: _____

Email: _____

Name: _____ Phone: _____

Email: _____

Name: _____ Phone: _____

Email: _____

Name: _____ Phone: _____

Email: _____

Checklist for Family Led Body Preparation

Bowls for bathing:
___

Candles:
___

Clothes:
___

Makeup:
___

Scarves and shawls:
___

Soap/shampoo:
___

Table for supplies:
___

Towels:
___

Washcloths:
___

Waterproof cover for table for body:
___

Sheets:
___

Blankets:
___

Pillow/pillowcases:
___

Scissors:
___

Checklist for Communication

Camera:
___

Computer/printer:
___

Contact list:
___

I Want You to Know

Notecards: _____

Paper/pens: _____

Paperwork: _____

Phone numbers: _____

Photo albums: _____

Scrapbooks: _____

Stapler: _____

Markers: _____

Other: _____

Personal Care Body Preparation

Clothing: _____

Jewelry: _____

Makeup: _____

After preparation, I would like my body lying in honor here:

For the wake area I would like

Candles: _____

Flowers: _____

Music: _____

Mementos: _____

Photographs: _____

Fragrances: _____

Oils: _____

Prayers: _____

Storytelling: _____

Other:

_____

_____

_____

_____

Finally, whether a funeral home is utilized for after death care or not, there are many duties and coordinating services that a third party can provide to make things easier for the grieving family.

Much like an event manager or "day of" coordinator can help a wedding or party run effortlessly, a mourning doula or mourning coordinator can help take stress out of the planning and execution of a wake, funeral, or social gathering after the services. There are a number of terms being used for those who offer paid services for attending to details of both families led death care and the time from death through final disposition. Canada is deep in the throes of legal battles at the writing of this book coming directly from the birth midwife industry regarding the use of the term "death midwife". They feel that to use the term "midwife" in any form is inappropriate unless there has been similar education and certification as they have had to complete to become certified birth midwives. As you search for someone to help, be aware that there are many terms being used and you may need to get a bit creative in your search.

In no way does this person take the place or substitute for a funeral director. This person takes care of all the behind the scenes coordination. You may also want to take the list I have provided below and divide it between family and friends that have volunteered to help you. Be sure to be very clear about each person's duties and double check to be sure that nothing falls through the cracks.

The flip side of hiring someone to coordinate is having family and friends take on all or some of these duties. There is solid reasoning behind choosing to have volunteers do these tasks, and I heartily recommend this path. As you are the one making these plans in advance, the details of your final time on earth are unknown. It can be perhaps comforting to you to have someone hired to help with these details afterward, or you may see the value in having other family members assist. These next few paragraphs are written in support of the one or ones who take care of you and hold vigil for you. You may want to print out or copy these next few pages and have them available to those that will be caring for you. Just remember that we heal through doing. It can be a positive experience to know that you helped with some of the logistics as a grieving family member. Having tasks to complete, to contribute to the process is a part of healing.

A Note to Caregivers:

As the final days and moments of death approach, as a caregiver, you may be utterly exhausted both physically and emotionally. You have held this vigil for some time with very little or no sleep, probably without proper hydration and sustenance, and certainly without healthy exercise. Your reserves are depleted. By now if you have been journeying with your loved one along the way, you have experienced a hundred small waves of grief. You have experienced grief with every small loss that has occurred along this path that may have lasted weeks, months, or years. You've been in the thick of the brave battle and have contributed everything you have to making the death of your loved one as "good" as possible. And now, the end arrives finding you feeling panicked that the weeks and months have come down to days or hours or minutes. You feel an unexplained pull to "do something." This is the very time that all you need to do is be present.

Simultaneously, waves of family and friends begin to arrive from nearby and far away. Many of these family members are feeling a tsunami of emotions as they arrive and see their loved one, perhaps for the first time, preparing to transition. They have not experienced your many small moments of grief, and suddenly, they find themselves knocked down by the huge wave that just hit them. As completely depleted as you are, in a flash you become the one comforting others instead of the other way around. You are making it "okay" for everyone else. If you are feeling angry and resentful, it is completely normal. Go ahead… be pissed off! Take a drive, a walk, a bubble bath, and use 30 minutes to regain your center.

By all means, understand that you will want to be present at the time of death. Much like the OB/Gyn wants to be present to birth the baby they have been monitoring for 9 months, you want to see this through because you have invested your time, your energy, your spirit, and your emotion. Many times when family members converge, the primary caregiver gets completely sidetracked with making beds, arranging transportation and meals, and managing so many tasks that they are not where they absolutely should be - by their loved one's side.

Here is another great opportunity for communication. Well ahead of time when possible, these conversations should be had with the entire family. To avoid surprises, hurt feelings, or misunderstandings, let it be known that you cherish that family is going to arrive when possible before death occurs, but your focus will continue to remain as it has been, on the one passing from this life. This is not the time to be a martyr or be self-effacing. Stand up for your place as the primary caregiver and continue to be the advocate for your loved one just as you have been all along this expedition. It is not your journey to take on any one's else's guilt, emotions, or issues. The love and care of the person you have been caring for should continue to be your priority. All these people know how to take care of themselves in their own lives. Don't feel you suddenly need to take over that role for them now. By this time, you are probably so exhausted that you are already walking into walls. Set the precedent before they even arrive, that you are not there to be their social director. I don't say this to be harsh. I say it to prompt you to be your own best advocate.

After the initial wall of grief that the newcomers will experience, the next response will probably be guilt. They experience the weight of all they have not done during this most stressful time. They come face to face with the reality of all you have done, the burdens you have shouldered and they are undoubtedly unhappy with themselves, even if they are not able to properly express it. This can be shown by catapulting into task overdrive, or finding fault with tiny things of no consequence, or retreating to another location. Below is a list of coordinator duties that are easily divided up among family and friends to let everyone feel that they are contributing to the tasks that need to be completed. You'll want to keep track of who is assigned to what tasks and have them report back to make sure that everything is done in a timely fashion. Allowing others to do something of substance to assist will help them feel better, and it will certainly help you feel a bit less burdened. When you are grief stricken, tired, headachy, and constantly trying to hold your emotions in check, the last thing you will want to do is come up with a job for each family member that comes at you with, "What can I do?" This list can be your cheat sheet to give your brain a little bit of a rest in those first hours both before and after the death of your family member.

Coordinator Duties

- Handle details of daily maintenance during the initial period including the viewing and/or reception following service

- Enlist help from others to run errands to bank, post office, groceries, etc.

- Clean dishes throughout each day

- Sort through and coordinate food donations

- Keep list of food donations for thank you notes

- Tape name and phone numbers on bottom of all dishes to returned

- Plan meals for family before and after the service

- Coordinate childcare through viewing, service, and reception

- Coordinate pet care through viewing, service, reception

- Coordinate house cleaning throughout, before, and following service

I Want You to Know

- Coordinate any small home repairs needed before service

- Coordinate lawn care before service

- Coordinate change of answering machine message to thank callers and to give service information

- Coordinate change of answering machine after disposition

- Answering of phone/taking and relaying of messages

- Make reservations for out of town guests

- Print out contact info for all area restaurants

- Write all information details to be kept by phone to relay callers

- Start time and location of all services

- Directions to all services

- What hotels and B&Bs are nearby

- What to wear, what to bring to house that may be needed

- Directions from airport, train station, bus station, etc.

- Details of death event (who was there, suffering, etc.)

Other duties:

_____

_____

_____

_____

I Want You to Know

Disclaimer: Note that things are vastly different if a death is unexpected or if a death happened outside the home. Please contact your local National Home Funeral Association to see what the legal requirements are and to help you navigate the choices that are best for the given situation.

Coordinator who will be serving as a family led death care guide:

Name:
_____

Phone:
_____

Email:
_____

Person named to oversee coordination of details

Name:
_____

Phone:
_____

People who have volunteered to help with details

Name:
_____

Phone:
_____

Name:
_____

Phone:
_____

Name:
_____

Phone:
_____

I Want You to Know

Name:
_____

Phone:
_____

Name:
_____

Phone:
_____

Name:
_____

Phone:
_____

The balance of funeral and memorial choices will be located in the next chapter.

I Want You to Know

*"Even death is not to be feared by
one who has lived wisely."*

~~Buddha

I Want You to Know

Funeral and Memorial Wishes

Alison was surprised to read a statistic that 81 percent of people responding said having a financial back up plan in the case of an emergency was very important, but only 45 percent said they had any plans and only 35 percent said they actually had funds on hand to meet their financial needs for three months or less. It took her back to the deaths of both her parents within a 5-year span and how blessed they had been as a family because of the forward thinking and planning of their mom and dad.

She remembers that her parents had always been organized and orderly. She and her brothers also vaguely remember a time in their childhood when their mother's father died unexpectedly when they were young. In addition to their mom being sad, they all have differing memories about heated phone conversations and both their parents sitting around the dining room table with mounds of paperwork for what seemed like a long time.

When they were all teenagers, her brother asked their Mom once about that time and why it felt so weird around the house and what all those papers were about. She didn't give many details, but the gist of the story was that her father had died with a will including little direction, owned property all over the place, had lots of debts and it was left up to her as the sole survivor to try and figure it all out. "Don't worry, that's never going to be the case in this household!" she said to Alison's brother with a quick hug.

When their father became ill in his 70's, the family had gathered at the house and were nestled in the downstairs den that had become his bedroom, either on his bed or in chairs up close beside him. Stories were being batted back and forth between the children and that bittersweet feeling of overwhelming love and sadness was thick in the room.

Alison remembers her dad quietly saying to anyone that would listen, "It's all taken care of you know." "What Dad, what is taken care of?" she asked him. "When I die, you kids and your mom don't need to worry about anything. Mom has an envelope with everything we both want for our funerals. It's all paid for. Everything's decided. We don't want you to have to worry about anything. We had too much worry in our lives with our families. We wanted it to stop with us. We hope you'll do the same. Take some of the money left from us and *do the same things for your families, ok?" Everyone patted the bed, or him, "Sure, Dad, sure thing."*

Alison admitted to me that she really didn't get it at the time. She was just focused on her dad still hoping he would rally and life would get back to normal. After his passing, the family was so immersed in the depth of his loss that she never really thought about details. The week of his death was a blur and her focus shifted to gathering enough strength to get back to work the next week and try to appear somewhat normal to the world while she was still reeling from grief inside.

About 5 years later, her mother was out with friends at lunch when she suffered a stroke. By the time the two closest siblings reached the hospital, their mother had died. When hospital personnel asked what funeral home they would like to use, Alison and her brother looked at each other with a blank stare. "Oh my God, you seriously think we can answer that question right now?" she snapped at the woman. Her brother looked at her, "There's an envelope, remember? Where do you think it is?" he asked Alison.

Their mother's morning coffee cup was sitting upside down on the dish strainer, with a short grocery list laying on the counter next to the strainer. Alison remembers going over and picking up the list and putting it in her pocket with the intention of getting the items for her mom and then suddenly feeling the tears hit her when she realized her mom would never need those things.

The envelope their dad talked about was on their mother's desk leaning against her mail file. Reluctantly, her brother opened the envelope and slid the contents out on to the desk. In the pile was everything they would need to know. There was a copy of both of their parents' advance directives, their parents' wills, the pre-need information with the funeral with everything pre-paid, what their Mom wanted to be dressed in, who she wanted notified, what she wanted read at the funeral, what music she wanted, and even a receipt and description of a luncheon to be provided by a local caterer for the family after burial.

Alison remembers, "We sat there together going through each and every token of our parents' love and care for us as we realized the time, effort, and energy it took them to plan every component of what we would have had to do, if they hadn't done it for us." I said to my brother, "And I snapped the head off that poor woman at the hospital because I couldn't even manage to think about what funeral home we would want to have Mom taken to. Imagine if we had had to do all this ourselves!"

The next few days were spent sitting out on my parents' deck or in their kitchen telling family stories, catching one another up on our own lives, and enjoying the visits of the friends and neighbors that stopped by. As everyone's families began to arrive for the service, the house filled even more with love and support. Alison was continually in awe of the gift of this time to just be free to cry, laugh, and enjoy her brothers and their families. Their biggest decision was what they would wear to the funeral, she remembers. It was just such a generous act of love from our Mom and Dad to us. And yes, we have all paid it forward to our families. Each one of us has developed a complete death plan with our spouses. In each of our envelopes is a story about our parents and what they did for us. When our kids read our packets, even though they've heard us talk about it, they will understand the depth of the love behind why we have provided this for them.

Disclaimer: This document is meant for personal planning purposes only. It is not meant to be substituted for a legal document in any way. Nothing within this document is meant to serve as medical or legal advice in any capacity.

Funerals and Memorials can be as simple or involved as you wish. The purpose here is to get you thinking about what you may like and, just as important, what you don't want. Feel free to add in notes at the end as there may be things you would like to include in addition to what is offered here.

A Note on direct burials:

Much like direct cremation, direct burial or immediate burial is the internment of a body in the first days following death. This, like direct cremation, is one of the most cost effective burial options and all funeral homes in the United States offer them.

Direct burial uses no embalming, no service, and no ceremony. They are less than half the price of traditional funerals because they do not include things like cosmetic preparation, viewings, and ceremonies.

I Want You to Know

Naturally, it is much easier to plan a direct burial as well. A memorial service can always be held at a time and location most convenient for you and your family. This can be ideal when a death occurred out-of-state.

As in direct cremation, this choice is not the best for everyone, but it is beneficial to be aware of all the options.

As we have done in previous chapters, we'll start with the basics.

Details of After Death Care:

I have a disposition container:
_____

It is paid for:
_____

Business/individual disposition container was purchased from

Name:
_____

Phone:
_____

Email:
_____

If you have not pre-purchased or chosen a disposition container fill out the following:

I would prefer a conventional casket

    Yes: _____ No: _____

Description:

    Pine box: _____ decorated: _____

    Shroud: _____ description: _____

    Cardboard: _____ decorated: _____

I Want You to Know

Objects/mementos placed inside:

_____

_____

_____

_____

_____

For Cremation:

Urn: _____ decorated: _____

Cardboard: _____ decorated: _____

Other: _____ description: _____

I wish to be embalmed (not normally required by law)

    Yes: _____ No: _____

I wish to have an autopsy (autopsies are only required at the medical examiners discretion in certain cases. You can choose to have an autopsy at the expense of your estate if desired)

    Yes: _____ No: _____

I wish to be buried*

    Yes: _____ No: _____

I wish for my body to be donated**

    Yes: _____ No: _____

I wish to be cremated***

    Yes: _____ No: _____

I Want You to Know

Please expand with further direction in the related sections below:

I have a pre-need funeral and burial contract

    Yes: _____ No: _____

Funeral Home:
_____

Phone:
_____

Address:
_____

Funeral Agent Contact:
_____

Where the paperwork for the pre-need can be found:
_____

I am a member of a cremation/funeral/memorial society:

Name:
_____

Address:
_____

Phone:
_____

Where the contract information be located:
_____

Insurance Policy to cover final disposition:

Company Name:
_____

Agent's Name:
_____

Phone:
_____

Policy Number:
_____

Policy location:

_____

*For Burial

Where do you wish to be buried?
_____

Do you want to be buried in the ground?

    Yes: _____ No: _____

Do you want to be buried in a mausoleum?

    Yes: _____ No: _____

I would like my casket placed inside a vault*

    Yes: _____ No: _____

* While never required by law, many cemeteries require the use of a vault to keep the ground of the cemetery level. However, you can save money (and cement) by using a grave liner which has a top and sides but no bottom. You can also request that a vault, if required, be installed upside down and with no lid if you prefer the idea of returning to the earth. If the cemetery or the town (if it is a town cemetery) insists that either a vault or grave liner is required, be sure to do further research. I can think of a certain MA town that told a woman she would have to have a vault only to find, when she looked into it more closely, the group that wrote the town law actually had no legal right to have written it in the first place.

    Do you have a purchased plot through your pre-need contract?

        Yes: _____ No: _____

Do you have a privately purchased funeral plot?

    Yes: _____ No: _____

Name, location and plot number:
_____

I Want You to Know

Where can the paperwork for this plot be found?
_____

I would like to be buried individually:
_____

I would like to be buried with a companion:
_____

Name:
_____
Contact, if living:
_____
Phone:
_____

I am eligible for burial in a Veteran's Cemetery

    Yes: _____ No: _____

    The paper work that proves I am eligible for burial in a Veteran's Cemetery can be found here:
_____

I have no preference where I am buried:
_____

**For Donation

Full body donation is a way to contribute to the advancement of treatments for many conditions. Alzheimer's, cancer, diabetes, MS, ALS, arthritis and degenerative joint disease, spinal injuries, heart disease, and infectious diseases are just some of the conditions that are researched because of body donation. Don't be confused; body donation and organ donation are two different things entirely. There are many myths and misunderstandings about the process of body donation. I highly recommend planning well in advance and researching all the available options and organizations. It is important to realize that there are circumstances that can happen that may make your body no longer eligible for donation. For this reason, always have a plan B to substitute should something happen that would change eligibility. There are a number of options for donation. Be sure to choose one that will use your body in a way that you would desire. Many people are drawn to full body donation due to the decreased cost of disposition. When you create your Plan B, include your thoughts on payment should your body not be eligible at the time of your death.

Organization for full body donation:
_____

Address:
_____

Phone:
_____

Back up disposition plan if no longer eligible for donation:

_____

_____

_____

_____

***For Cremation

Cremation is part of my pre-need funeral and burial contract

    Yes: _____ No: _____

I desire direct cremation*

    Yes: _____ No: _____

There is no viewing or funeral with direct cremation

I would like a memorial sometime following my direct cremation

    Yes: _____ No: _____

I wish for a standard cremation

I Want You to Know

       Yes: _____ No: _____

I wish for alkaline hydrolysis cremation*

       Yes: _____ No: _____

* Not readily available everywhere

I wish to have witnesses to my cremation

       Yes: _____ No: _____

I would like the witnesses to be:

Name: _____ Phone: _____

Name: _____ Phone: _____

Name: _____ Phone: _____

Name: _____ Phone: _____

Name: _____ Phone: _____

I would like my ashes returned

       Yes: _____ No: _____

I would like my ashes returned to:

Name:
_____

Phone:
_____

I would like my ashes scattered

       Yes: _____ No: _____

I would like my ashes scattered here:
_____

*Be aware of local ordinances regarding the spreading of ashes. No, there are no ash-spreading police, but it is respectful to obey local protocol. There is no health, safety or environmental issue to be concerned about. Clearly if you desire to spread ashes on private property, you will want to obtain permission from the owner in advance. I would recommend getting it in writing. On controlled public lands such as public city parks, there will be rules and regulations and permit requirements. If you are planning on scattering ashes at sea, or desire to spread them at the shore, be sure to research what is required. In the United States, all ashes should be spread at least three nautical miles from shore. In addition, you are required to file with the EPA within 30 days.

I would like my ashes scattered by:

Name: _____ Phone: _____

Name: _____ Phone: _____

Name: _____ Phone: _____

Name: _____ Phone: _____

Name: _____ Phone: _____

Name: _____ Phone: _____

Name: _____ Phone: _____

I would like my ashes buried

    Yes: _____ No: _____

I would like my ashes buried here:
_____

I would like my ashes buried individually

    Yes: _____ No: _____

I Want You to Know

        I would like my ashes to be buried with a companion:

        Yes: _____ No: _____

Companion Name:
_____

Contact, if living:
_____

Phone:
_____

I have no preference where my ashes are buried:
_____

Cemetery Markers

    Cemeteries will sometimes dictate what kinds of markers can be used. Be sure to confirm with your desired cemetery ahead of time to avoid unpleasant surprises down the road.

    I would like this kind of marker:

_____ upright
_____ flat
_____ monument/statue
_____ no preference
_____ Other, description:
_____ I am eligible for and would like a veteran's marker

The papers that prove my eligibility are located:

I would like the inscription on my headstone to read:

_____

_____

_____

_____

I Want You to Know

"I am always saddened by the death of a good person. It is from this sadness that a feeling of gratitude emerges. I feel honored to have known them and blessed that their passing serves as a reminder to me that my time on this beautiful earth is limited and that I should seize the opportunity I have to forgive, share, explore, and love. I can think of no greater way to honor the deceased than to live this way."

~~Steve Maraboli

I Want You to Know

Eulogy Notes

I believe that every person who has ever been to a funeral has caught themselves thinking at some time or other when listening to a eulogy, "I wonder what people would say about me?" We wonder what people would remember about us, and what stories they would tell.

I've also been at a memorial and felt disappointed because something that I thought was an important fact or memorable story was left out of the eulogy. You know how that happens, don't you? After we experience the death of someone close to us, we are overcome with emotions. Sometimes we actually bypass emotion and land in a state of complete zone out. Either way, we cannot remember facts or recall important stories in the same manner we would when we were in a stress-free frame of mind.

If you like, you can take the information you will gather in this section and actually write your own eulogy! I know, it does seem rather strange to consider, doesn't it? Conceptually, it does make sense if you have the fortitude to do it. At the very least, having all these important facts in one location will make your loved ones most thankful when the time arrives for the writing of your eulogy.

A wonderful benefit of this section will be the gift of history to your family. Children, grandchildren, nieces, and nephews will learn things about you that they never knew before. They may be inspired to begin to document their own life stories. Sadly, family histories are being lost as our older generation dies. This is a wonderful way to make sure your family history is preserved.

It may seem odd to start with "birth stories" because how many people remember the story of their own birth? I have no idea about the birth stories of my siblings, but my birth story was talked about often enough for me to enjoy the unique circumstances. I was born during an unusual Spring blizzard in North Eastern Ohio. My Dad plowed the driveway, bundled Mom into the car only to already be snowed in again. He was forced to get out, shovel a little way, get back in the car, move forward a bit, and repeat. It took him long enough to make his way up the drive that they weren't sure they'd make it to the hospital in time. What grandchild wouldn't get a kick out of hearing a story like that?

If you don't know anything about your birth story, or that of a sibling, you may have some great memories to share about your own children's births.

~~~~~~

Notes to someone reading this to gain information on writing a eulogy: Delivering the eulogy is a wonderful way to be a part of the service of someone that is dear to you. Remembering to focus on the one who has died instead of your own nerves and anxiety will help you dig more deeply to write a heartfelt tribute. No matter how well you know the person that has died, and no matter how great the notes may be in this chapter to help you gain information, be sure to sit down with family and close friends to allow them to tell their personal stories. Just the experience of remembering important events and sharing them together is a very important part of the beginning of the healing journey.

When you are ready to start the writing process, take some time to brainstorm. The best way is to allow yourself a set amount of time to free write. Free writing is when you take pen to paper and literally write whatever comes to your mind about the person you are going to write the eulogy for. Don't edit, don't worry about punctuation, just write. Many times there will be sparks of inspiration within that blast of words that you might not have uncovered otherwise.

Frequently this will happen organically, but look for a theme within your first writings, and then begin your first draft from that perspective. It could be something like, "All the many sides of", "Where would we have been without", "She was the gardener of her life", "The center of his world was the kitchen", etc. Having a theme helps set the pictures of your story into the listeners' minds and will enable them to hold on to a more vibrant memory of your words. It also helps you, the writer, obtain a literary flow in your writing.

If you feel that there are personal issues in the family that have yet to be resolved, remember that this is not the place to do that. This should be respectful and kind. You can be honest in the spirit of your writing without adding hurtful details or trying to settle old scores. If this really is a brick wall for you, the delivery of the eulogy should be handled by another person.

I Want You to Know

It's good to start with illustrating the theme of your eulogy, and if you a have story that will do that, all the better. This first draft is still really fluid, so don't get bogged down in the minutia at this point.

Step away for some time after you finish. When you come back and read it through, you'll find that many of the ideas you started will naturally finish themselves as you re-read your work. Do this as many times as it takes, and then go back to do a final check for grammar and spelling.

Be sure to write your eulogy legibly or print it out in large text that you can still read in subdued lighting and if tears are affecting your focus. Have tissues handy and a glass of water or a cough drop in case your throat becomes dry. And, yes, tears are fine. Don't worry if you need to stop for a moment and gather yourself. As you speak, project your voice not down to your written pages but up and over the heads of everyone in the room. You will speak to the farthest person in the farthest space of the room and that will assure that everyone in between can hear your words. Do this by taking just a moment as you step up to the podium to raise your head and set your eyes on your visual point before you say the first word. Remind yourself that your goal is to speak to that person so everyone will be able to hear you. I was so sad recently to be at the funeral of an old family friend that was so well attended the main salon was full, as was the entry hall, and two side rooms had been set up with closed circuit television and speakers. Not only was the picture so blurry I could barely identify who was speaking (how is that possible in 2016?), but when the eulogy was given, the person delivering their words was looking down at their paper and speaking quite softly. I don't imagine the first three rows of guests could hear his words, much less everyone else. How sad to leave all those people feeling empty after coming together to celebrate the life of a beautiful woman, a true matriarch!

Can the eulogy be humorous? A good case in point would be the infamous eulogy to Graham Chapman of Monty Python by John Cleese. If you are remembering the life of a particularly funny person that embodied humor, I would say the best way to honor them would be with humor in their eulogy. The key is to capture their essence. I remember watching the moving and emotional eulogy that Brooke Shields delivered at the funeral of Michael Jackson. To see him through Brooke's eyes was incredibly touching.

I Want You to Know

Remember at the beginning of these notes I said that it is helpful to focus on the one who had died, not on your nervousness? Keep that in mind as you prepare to speak. Remember that you want to help ease the burden of the family and friends present. You are honored to be the one to tell a story, so slow down, breathe deeply, make eye contact, and talk to the people in the room. Don't rush through just to be finished. Center yourself into the gift of your words and deliver them with love.

Below are some writing prompts:

Birth Stories:

_____

_____

_____

_____

_____

_____

_____

_____

_____

_____

_____

_____

_____

_____

I Want You to Know

Childhood Memories:

_____
_____
_____
_____
_____
_____
_____
_____
_____
_____
_____
_____
_____
_____
_____
_____
_____

I Want You to Know

School Days:

I Want You to Know

Sibling/Family Stories:

I Want You to Know

Career:

I Want You to Know

Significant Others:

I Want You to Know

Volunteering Stories:

I Want You to Know

Military Memories:

I Want You to Know

Interest/Hobbies/Vocations:

_____
_____
_____
_____
_____
_____
_____
_____
_____
_____
_____
_____
_____
_____
_____
_____
_____
_____
_____
_____

I Want You to Know

Best Joke I Know:

I Want You to Know

Funniest Thing I Remember:

I Want You to Know

Favorite Book or Movie and Why:

_____
_____
_____
_____
_____
_____
_____
_____
_____
_____
_____
_____
_____
_____
_____
_____
_____

I Want You to Know

Favorite Scripture Verse, Quote, or Song:

I Want You to Know

What I Want People to Remember About Me:

_____
_____
_____
_____
_____
_____
_____
_____
_____
_____
_____
_____
_____
_____
_____
_____
_____
_____
_____

I Want You to Know

Stories about my children:

I Want You to Know

People Who Made a Difference in My Life and Why:

I Want You to Know

What Really Matters:

I Want You to Know

"Not all of us can do great things.

But we can do small things with great love."

~~ Mother Teresa

Life Inventory

Although this chapter may feel redundant, I felt compelled to add this opportunity for a life review should you so choose.

Much of the work that has preceded this chapter may have been done when you are in a healthy period of your life as a way to be proactive for future days. Planning ahead and preparing the way for your family and friends to be able to do the work of honoring you by knowing your every wish when you face a major illness or death.

This life review is also known as an ethical will, life inventory, or legacy letter. It is not a legal document and has nothing to do with distribution of your assets. This is a way to share your personal values, the lessons you have learned in this life, the blessings you have experienced, and your hopes and dreams for your loved ones. You may even choose to include forgiveness to those close to you or your community that you feel has wronged you in the past, or to ask for forgiveness from someone. This chapter is to serve as your life inventory, which is to say, a way to convey your most important memories and life lessons to those that are closest to you. You can write one at any time. You may choose to include one now, and write another as you enter your later years.

This concept is not new. There are references to the tradition of ethical wills or legacy letters in both the Hebrew and the Christian Bible and in other cultures. Many people choose to write an ethical will, or life review at transitional periods in their lives and also when they are facing especially challenging life situations. Once written, they are to be shared with your loved ones and community while you are still living.

Here are a few writing prompts to get your thoughts flowing should you need them:

*Your personal life lessons
*Your personal life blessings
*Your largest life challenge
*Your beliefs and personal values
*Your spiritual values
*Your thoughts on love

I Want You to Know

*Asking and/or giving forgiveness
*What three things would you most want the next generation to know?

My legacy letter:

_____

_____

_____

_____

_____

_____

_____

_____

_____

_____

_____

_____

_____

_____

_____

_____

_____

_____

_____

_____

I Want You to Know

There is one final area for personal notes after this page. But before I say good bye, I wanted to convey some closing thoughts.

I applaud you for working your way through this guide! How do you feel? Have you remembered things you haven't thought of in years? Do you feel more centered and ready for whatever the future may bring? Do you feel compelled to provide a workbook for every family member?

You've done significant work within these pages. You are now part of a very powerful group of people. You are a change-maker and have created a wonderful legacy for those that care most for you.

Thank you for your courage. Thank you for impacting not only the lives of those that will care for you, but for the generation that will follow. They will learn more by your example than you may ever even know.

I encourage you to send me a letter or email to let me know your thoughts on this book and how filling out this information has affected you. Your feedback will help us further serve those that are serving others through caregiving. I can be reached at leslie@thevisionarypassage.com. I look forward to hearing from you.

I wish you love, laughter, and abundant legacies.

~~Leslie Cottrell Simonds

I Want You to Know

Personal Notes

Please use these last pages to add any additional notes that you may think of as you work your way through this book. At the request of my brilliant virtual assistant/daughter, we are leaving these pages' blank to allow for artistic expression in addition to the written word.

I Want You to Know

I Want You to Know

I Want You to Know

www.ingramcontent.com/pod-product-compliance
Lightning Source LLC
Chambersburg PA
CBHW080655190526
45169CB00006B/2123